This Letters to my Dog in Heaven

IS DEDICATED TO:

_____

How To Use This Letters To My Dog In Heaven Keepsake Log Book:

This ultimate letter to my dog in heaven notebook is a perfect way to track and record all your favorite pet memories. This unique dog memory notebook is a great way to keep all of your keepsake information all in one place.

Each interior page includes prompts and space to record the following:

1. My Favorite Co-Woofer - Write the memories of the dog's arrival in the journal notes.

2. Paw Print Journal - Write out all the things you imagine what your favorite dog is doing right now in heaven, and important memories of spending time at home.

3. Favorite Dog Park - Construct your love letter and the heart feels you'd like to share..and the fun times at the dog park... so as to be reminded later when reminiscing...

4. Times you made me laugh so hard - Record funny, silly and important events about your favorite dog...

5. Favorite place to poop - Stay on task using this space to remember all the preferred places that silly pooch liked to poop.....come back here later to have a good laugh...

6. Photo Page - Space to put pictures in so to remember all the good times and that cute face...

If you are missing your favorite dog right now, this Letters to my Dog In Heaven planner and journal is a must have! Can make an awesome gift for the dog lover, and will be a keepsake memory forever.

Bless!

Letters to my dog in heaven

Dear Co-Woofer, thanks for being my supportive four-legged "co-worker" and I wanted to tell you that I love...

You were my favorite co-woofer, right now I'd like to tell you...

Today you make me happy by remembering your favorite...

Today, you make me happy by...

Your favorite dog park was...

Favorite place to get your dog bath was...

Your rating in the Snuggles department was...
☆ ☆ ☆ ☆ ☆

Your favorite toy was...

The times you made me laughed so hard were...

I found it funny when you...

I loved it when you...

When you rolled over, you...

On our "break time" from work, you loved to...

At the dog parked, you hate...

At the dog parked, you like..

Some lessons I learned from knowing you are...

Your favorite place to be scratched was....

Favorite place to poop was....

Your favorite place to nap was...

Favorite TV show was...

My "support system" includes...

You loved to torture the...

Things I loved

- [ ] Squeaky toys
- [ ] Bath time
- [ ] The vet
- [ ] Being a good boy
- [ ] Playtime at the dog park
- [ ] Chewy toys
- [ ] Dog bones
- [ ] Treats for being cute
- [ ] Rubbing tail in owner's face
- [ ] Pawing for attention
- [ ] Sitting on the keyboard
- [ ] Kissing my owner's neck
- [ ] "Meetings" with my new manager at home
- [ ] Holding my owner's paws
- [ ] Receiving the max amount of petting i can get
- [ ] Personal lap warmer
- [ ] Gossiping with my co-woofer
- [ ] Trying to drink my owner's coffee while sitting on the laptop
- [ ] Accidentally adding bookmarks to my owner's computer because i want attention

Letters to my dog in heaven

Dear Co-Woofer, thanks for being my supportive four-legged "co-worker" and I wanted to tell you that I love...

You were my favorite co-woofer, right now I'd like to tell you...

Today you make me happy by remembering your favorite...

Today, you make me happy by...

Your favorite dog park was... Favorite place to get your dog bath was... Your rating in the Snuggles department was...
☆☆☆☆☆

Your favorite toy was... The times you made me laughed so hard were...

I found it funny when you... I loved it when you... When you rolled over, you...

On our "break time" from work, you loved to...

At the dog parked, you hate...

At the dog parked, you like..

Some lessons I learned from knowing you are...

Your favorite place to be scratched was.... Favorite place to poop was.... Your favorite place to nap was...

Favorite TV show was... My "support system" includes... You loved to torture the...

Things I loved

- [ ] Squeaky toys
- [ ] Bath time
- [ ] The vet
- [ ] Being a good boy
- [ ] Playtime at the dog park
- [ ] Chewy toys
- [ ] Dog bones
- [ ] Treats for being cute
- [ ] Rubbing tail in owner's face
- [ ] Pawing for attention
- [ ] Sitting on the keyboard
- [ ] Kissing my owner's neck
- [ ] "Meetings" with my new manager at home
- [ ] Holding my owner's paws
- [ ] Receiving the max amount of petting i can get
- [ ] Personal lap warmer
- [ ] Gossiping with my co-woofer
- [ ] Trying to drink my owner's coffee while sitting on the laptop
- [ ] Accidentally adding bookmarks to my owner's computer because i want attention

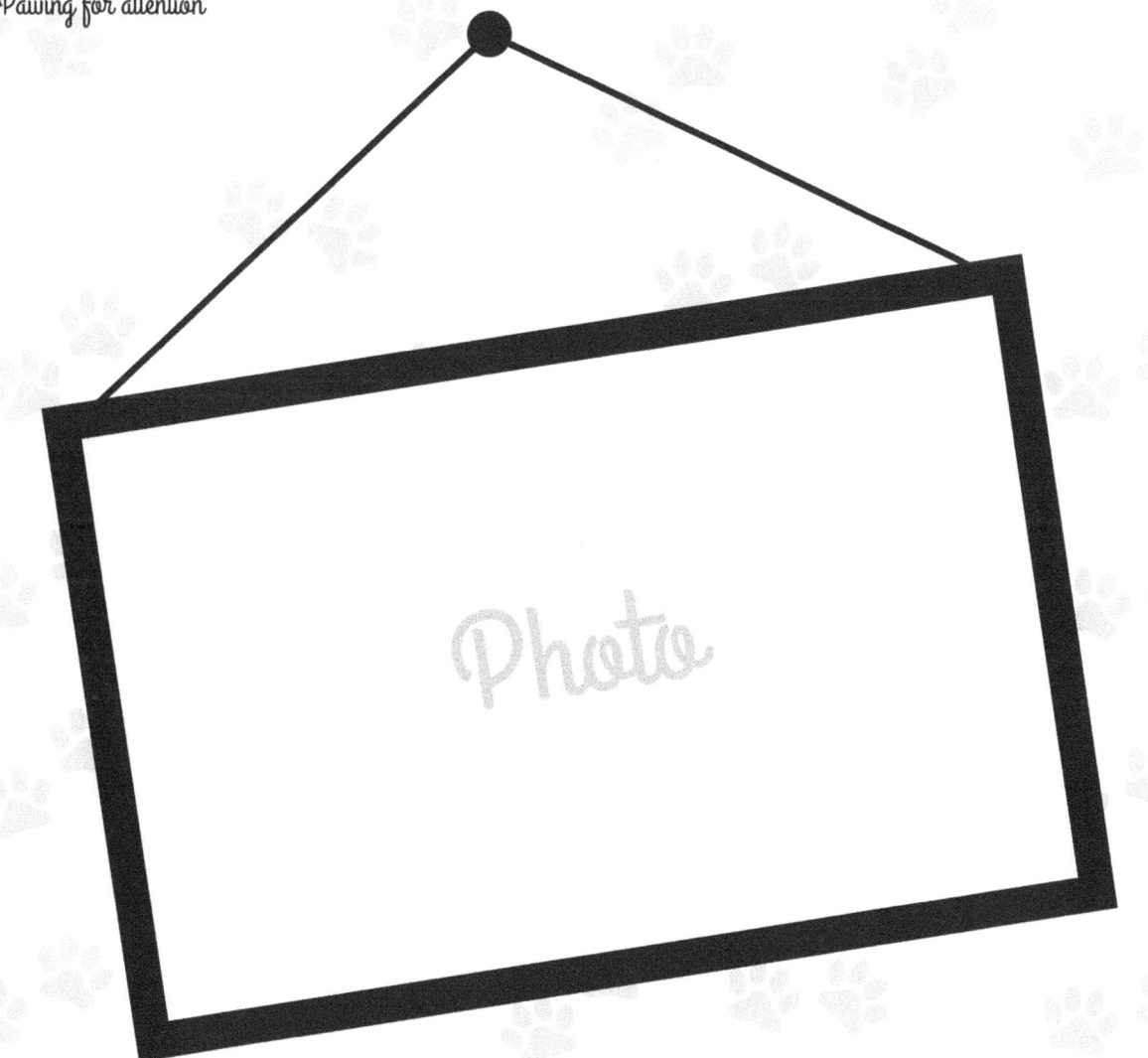

Letters to my dog in heaven

Dear Co-Woofer, thanks for being my supportive four-legged "co-worker" and I wanted to tell you that I love...

You were my favorite co-woofer, right now I'd like to tell you...

Today you make me happy by remembering your favorite...

Today, you make me happy by...

Your favorite dog park was...

Favorite place to get your dog bath was...

Your rating in the Snuggles department was... ☆☆☆☆☆

Your favorite toy was...

The times you made me laughed so hard were...

I found it funny when you...

I loved it when you...

When you rolled over, you...

On our "break time" from work, you loved to...

At the dog parked, you hate...

At the dog parked, you like..

Some lessons I learned from knowing you are...

Your favorite place to be scratched was....

Favorite place to poop was....

Your favorite place to nap was...

Favorite TV show was...

My "support system" includes...

You loved to torture the...

Things I loved

- [ ] Squeaky toys
- [ ] Bath time
- [ ] The vet
- [ ] Being a good boy
- [ ] Playtime at the dog park
- [ ] Chewy toys
- [ ] Dog bones
- [ ] Treats for being cute
- [ ] Rubbing tail in owner's face
- [ ] Pawing for attention
- [ ] Sitting on the keyboard
- [ ] Kissing my owner's neck
- [ ] "Meetings" with my new manager at home
- [ ] Holding my owner's paws
- [ ] Receiving the max amount of petting i can get
- [ ] Personal lap warmer
- [ ] Gossiping with my co-woofer
- [ ] Trying to drink my owner's coffee while sitting on the laptop
- [ ] Accidentally adding bookmarks to my owner's computer because i want attention

Letters to my dog in heaven

Dear Co-Woofer, thanks for being my supportive four-legged "co-worker" and I wanted to tell you that I love...

You were my favorite co-woofer, right now I'd like to tell you...

Today you make me happy by remembering your favorite...

Today, you make me happy by...

Your favorite dog park was... | Favorite place to get your dog bath was... | Your rating in the Snuggles department was... ☆☆☆☆☆

Your favorite toy was... | The times you made me laughed so hard were...

I found it funny when you... | I loved it when you... | When you rolled over, you...

On our "break time" from work, you loved to...

At the dog parked, you hate...

At the dog parked, you like..

Some lessons I learned from knowing you are...

Your favorite place to be scratched was.... | Favorite place to poop was.... | Your favorite place to nap was...

Favorite TV show was... | My "support system" includes... | You loved to torture the...

Things I loved

- ☐ Squeaky toys
- ☐ Bath time
- ☐ The vet
- ☐ Being a good boy
- ☐ Playtime at the dog park
- ☐ Chewy toys
- ☐ Dog bones
- ☐ Treats for being cute
- ☐ Rubbing tail in owner's face
- ☐ Pawing for attention
- ☐ Sitting on the keyboard
- ☐ Kissing my owner's neck
- ☐ "Meetings" with my new manager at home
- ☐ Holding my owner's paws
- ☐ Receiving the max amount of petting i can get
- ☐ Personal lap warmer
- ☐ Gossiping with my co-woofer
- ☐ Trying to drink my owner's coffee while sitting on the laptop
- ☐ Accidentally adding bookmarks to my owner's computer because i want attention

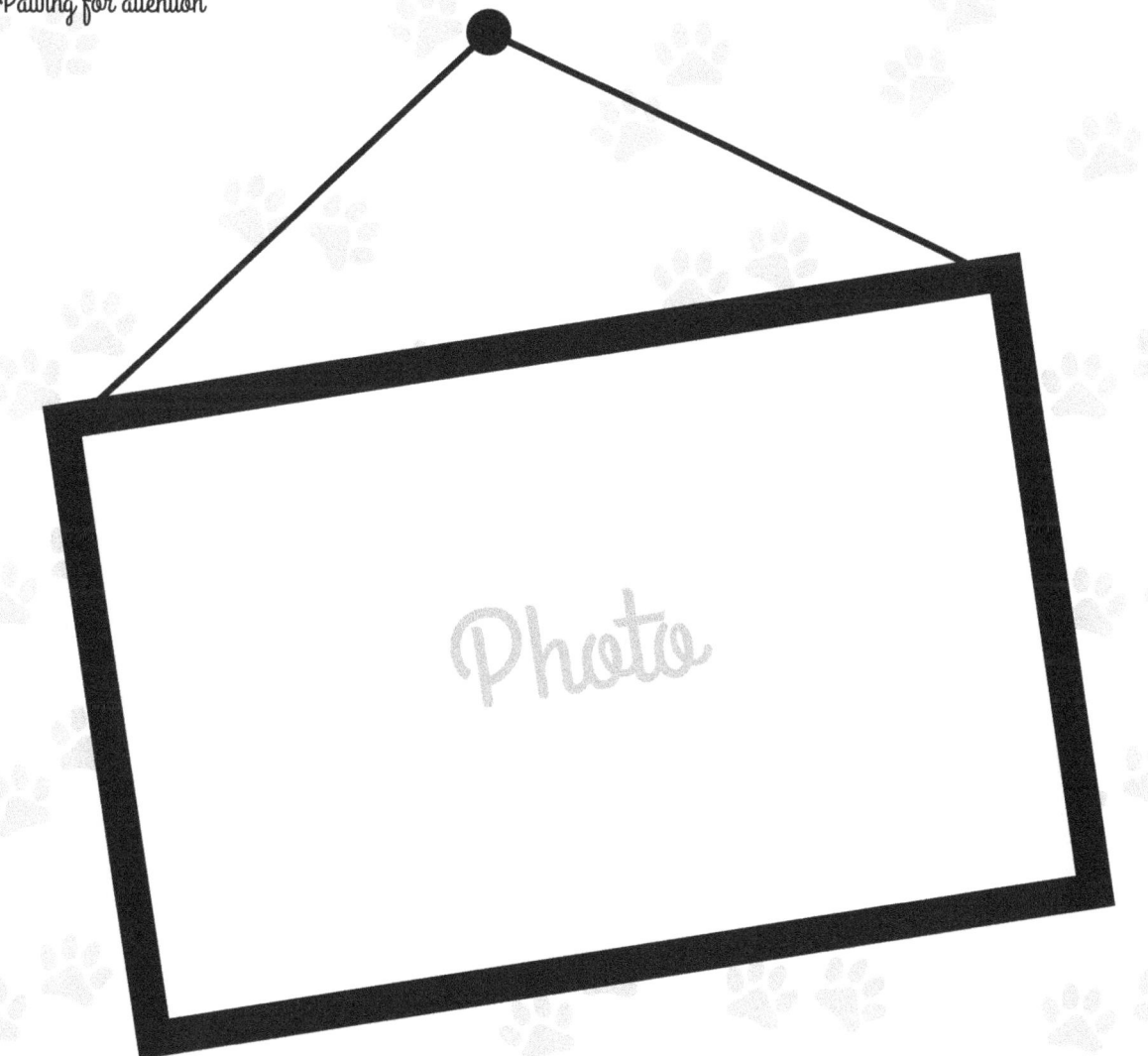

Letters to my dog in heaven

Dear Co-Woofer, thanks for being my supportive four-legged "co-worker" and I wanted to tell you that I love...

You were my favorite co-woofer, right now I'd like to tell you...

Today you make me happy by remembering your favorite...

Today, you make me happy by...

Your favorite dog park was...

Favorite place to get your dog bath was...

Your rating in the Snuggles department was... ☆☆☆☆☆

Your favorite toy was...

The times you made me laughed so hard were...

I found it funny when you...

I loved it when you...

When you rolled over, you...

On our "break time" from work, you loved to...

At the dog parked, you hate...

At the dog parked, you like..

Some lessons I learned from knowing you are...

Your favorite place to be scratched was....

Favorite place to poop was....

Your favorite place to nap was...

Favorite TV show was...

My "support system" includes...

You loved to torture the...

Things I loved

- [ ] Squeaky toys
- [ ] Bath time
- [ ] The vet
- [ ] Being a good boy
- [ ] Playtime at the dog park
- [ ] Chewy toys
- [ ] Dog bones
- [ ] Treats for being cute
- [ ] Rubbing tail in owner's face
- [ ] Pawing for attention
- [ ] Sitting on the keyboard
- [ ] Kissing my owner's neck
- [ ] "Meetings" with my new manager at home
- [ ] Holding my owner's paws
- [ ] Receiving the max amount of petting i can get
- [ ] Personal lap warmer
- [ ] Gossiping with my co-woofer
- [ ] Trying to drink my owner's coffee while sitting on the laptop
- [ ] Accidentally adding bookmarks to my owner's computer because i want attention

Letters to my dog in heaven

Dear Co-Woofer, thanks for being my supportive four-legged "co-worker" and I wanted to tell you that I love...

You were my favorite co-woofer, right now I'd like to tell you...

Today you make me happy by remembering your favorite...

Today, you make me happy by...

Your favorite dog park was...

Favorite place to get your dog bath was...

Your rating in the Snuggles department was...
☆☆☆☆☆

Your favorite toy was...

The times you made me laughed so hard were...

I found it funny when you...

I loved it when you...

When you rolled over, you...

On our "break time" from work, you loved to...

At the dog parked, you hate...

At the dog parked, you like..

Some lessons I learned from knowing you are...

Your favorite place to be scratched was....

Favorite place to poop was....

Your favorite place to nap was...

Favorite TV show was...

My "support system" includes...

You loved to torture the...

Things I loved

- ☐ Squeaky toys
- ☐ Bath time
- ☐ The vet
- ☐ Being a good boy
- ☐ Playtime at the dog park
- ☐ Chewy toys
- ☐ Dog bones
- ☐ Treats for being cute
- ☐ Rubbing tail in owner's face
- ☐ Pawing for attention
- ☐ Sitting on the keyboard
- ☐ Kissing my owner's neck
- ☐ "Meetings" with my new manager at home
- ☐ Holding my owner's paws
- ☐ Receiving the max amount of petting i can get
- ☐ Personal lap warmer
- ☐ Gossiping with my co-woofer
- ☐ Trying to drink my owner's coffee while sitting on the laptop
- ☐ Accidentally adding bookmarks to my owner's computer because i want attention

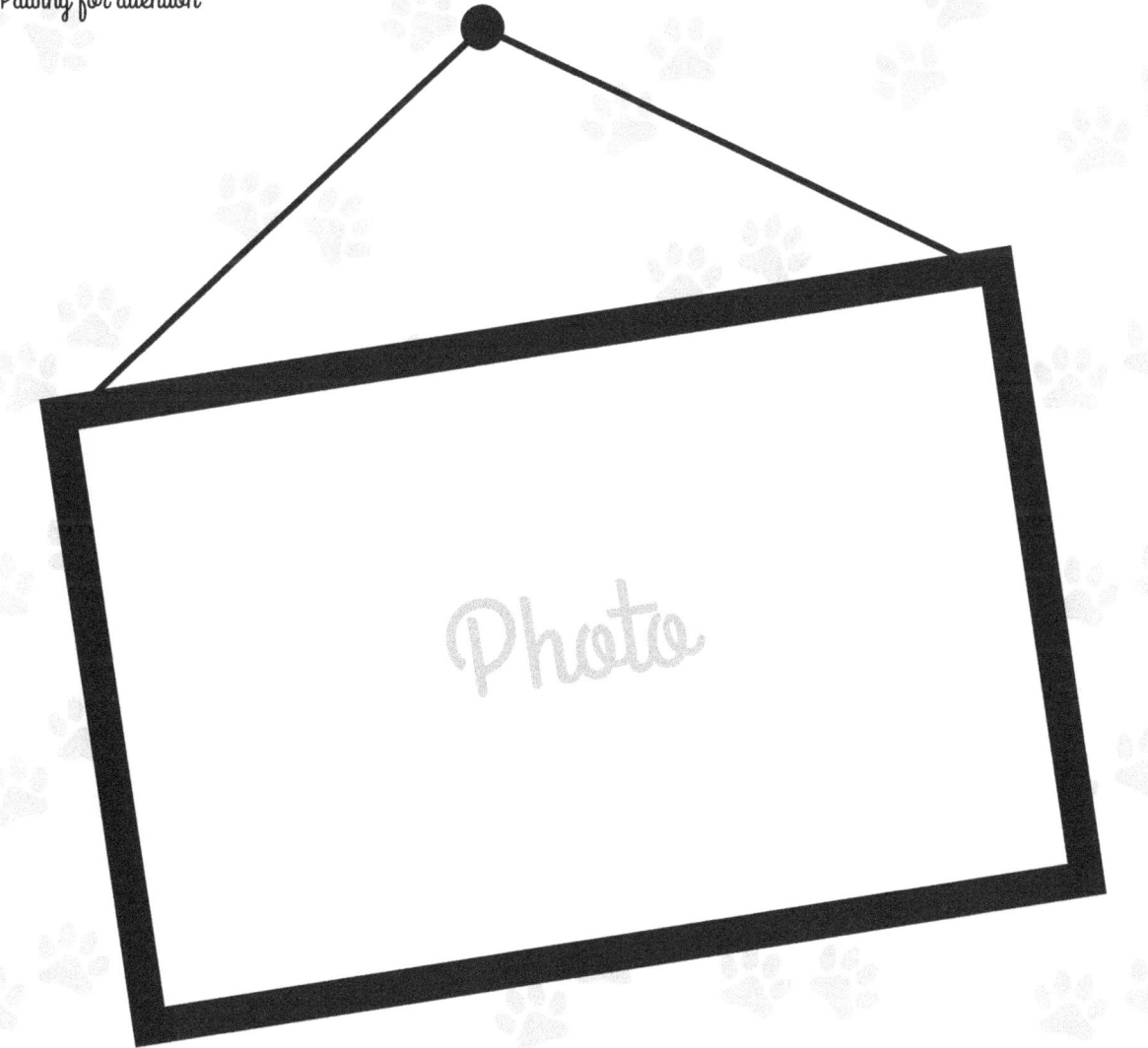

Letters to my dog in heaven

Dear Co-Woofer, thanks for being my supportive four-legged "co-worker" and I wanted to tell you that I love...

You were my favorite co-woofer, right now I'd like to tell you...

Today you make me happy by remembering your favorite...

Today, you make me happy by...

Your favorite dog park was...	Favorite place to get your dog bath was...	Your rating in the Snuggles department was... ☆☆☆☆☆

Your favorite toy was...	The times you made me laughed so hard were...

I found it funny when you...	I loved it when you...	When you rolled over, you...

On our "break time" from work, you loved to...

At the dog parked, you hate...

At the dog parked, you like..

Some lessons I learned from knowing you are...

Your favorite place to be scratched was....	Favorite place to poop was....	Your favorite place to nap was...

Favorite TV show was...	My "support system" includes...	You loved to torture the...

Things I loved

- ☐ Squeaky toys
- ☐ Bath time
- ☐ The vet
- ☐ Being a good boy
- ☐ Playtime at the dog park
- ☐ Chewy toys
- ☐ Dog bones
- ☐ Treats for being cute
- ☐ Rubbing tail in owner's face
- ☐ Pawing for attention
- ☐ Sitting on the keyboard
- ☐ Kissing my owner's neck
- ☐ "Meetings" with my new manager at home
- ☐ Holding my owner's paws
- ☐ Receiving the max amount of petting i can get
- ☐ Personal lap warmer
- ☐ Gossiping with my co-woofer
- ☐ Trying to drink my owner's coffee while sitting on the laptop
- ☐ Accidentally adding bookmarks to my owner's computer because i want attention

Letters to my dog in heaven

Dear Co-Woofer, thanks for being my supportive four-legged "co-worker" and I wanted to tell you that I love...

You were my favorite co-woofer, right now I'd like to tell you...

Today you make me happy by remembering your favorite...

Today, you make me happy by...

Your favorite dog park was...

Favorite place to get your dog bath was...

Your rating in the Snuggles department was...

☆ ☆ ☆ ☆ ☆

Your favorite toy was...

The times you made me laughed so hard were...

I found it funny when you...

I loved it when you...

When you rolled over, you...

On our "break time" from work, you loved to...

At the dog parked, you hate...

At the dog parked, you like..

Some lessons I learned from knowing you are...

Your favorite place to be scratched was....

Favorite place to poop was....

Your favorite place to nap was...

Favorite TV show was...

My "support system" includes...

You loved to torture the...

Things I loved

- [ ] Squeaky toys
- [ ] Bath time
- [ ] The vet
- [ ] Being a good boy
- [ ] Playtime at the dog park
- [ ] Chewy toys
- [ ] Dog bones
- [ ] Treats for being cute
- [ ] Rubbing tail in owner's face
- [ ] Pawing for attention
- [ ] Sitting on the keyboard
- [ ] Kissing my owner's neck
- [ ] "Meetings" with my new manager at home
- [ ] Holding my owner's paws
- [ ] Receiving the max amount of petting i can get
- [ ] Personal lap warmer
- [ ] Gossiping with my co-woofer
- [ ] Trying to drink my owner's coffee while sitting on the laptop
- [ ] Accidentally adding bookmarks to my owner's computer because i want attention

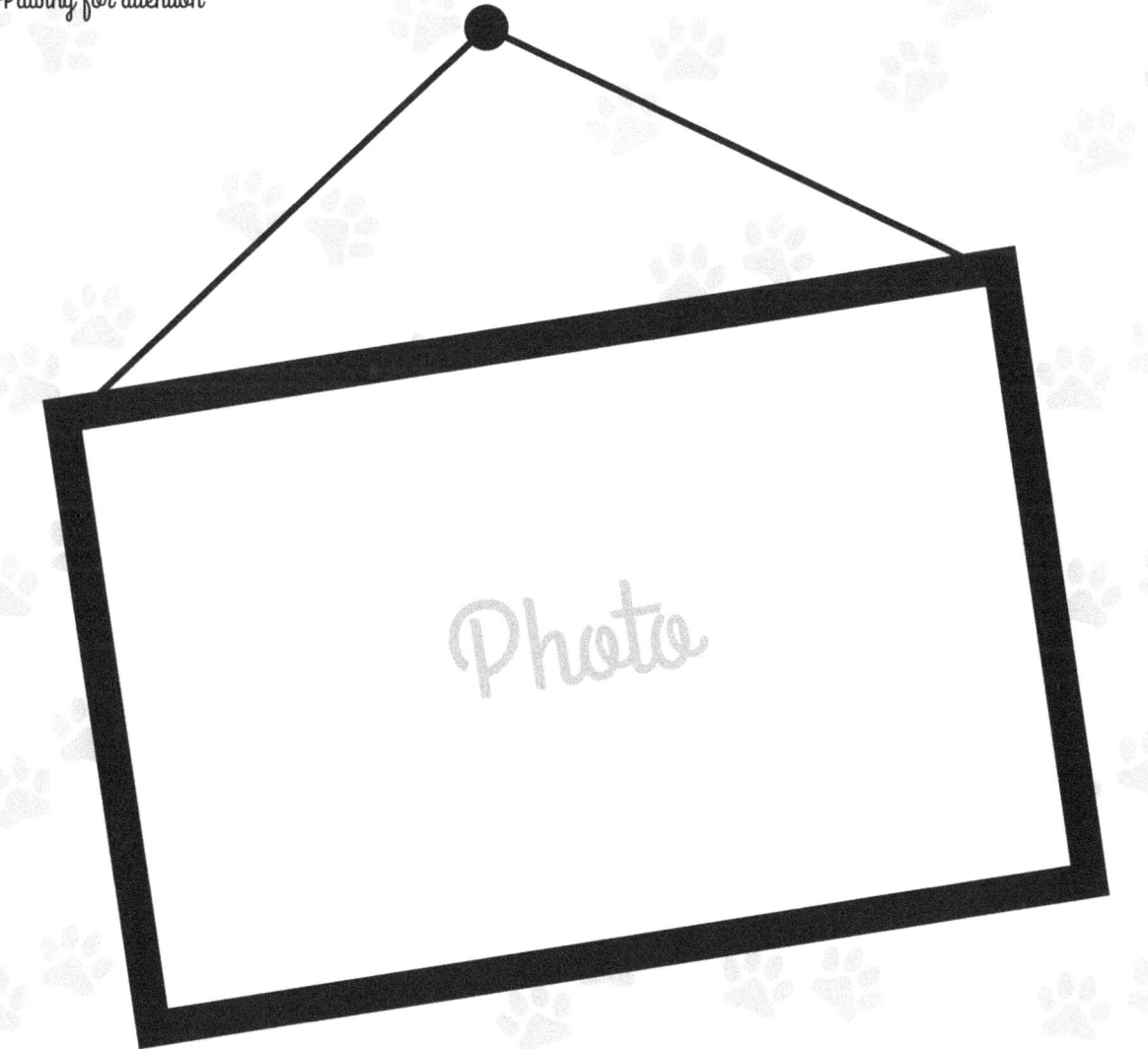

Letters to my dog in heaven

Dear Co-Woofer, thanks for being my supportive four-legged "co-worker" and I wanted to tell you that I love...

You were my favorite co-woofer, right now I'd like to tell you...

Today you make me happy by remembering your favorite...

Today, you make me happy by...

Your favorite dog park was...

Favorite place to get your dog bath was...

Your rating in the Snuggles department was... ☆☆☆☆☆

Your favorite toy was...

The times you made me laughed so hard were...

I found it funny when you...

I loved it when you...

When you rolled over, you...

On our "break time" from work, you loved to...

At the dog parked, you hate...

At the dog parked, you like..

Some lessons I learned from knowing you are...

Your favorite place to be scratched was....

Favorite place to poop was....

Your favorite place to nap was...

Favorite TV show was...

My "support system" includes...

You loved to torture the...

Things I loved

- ☐ Squeaky toys
- ☐ Bath time
- ☐ The vet
- ☐ Being a good boy
- ☐ Playtime at the dog park
- ☐ Chewy toys
- ☐ Dog bones
- ☐ Treats for being cute
- ☐ Rubbing tail in owner's face
- ☐ Pawing for attention
- ☐ Sitting on the keyboard
- ☐ Kissing my owner's neck
- ☐ "Meetings" with my new manager at home
- ☐ Holding my owner's paws
- ☐ Receiving the max amount of petting i can get
- ☐ Personal lap warmer
- ☐ Gossiping with my co-woofer
- ☐ Trying to drink my owner's coffee while sitting on the laptop
- ☐ Accidentally adding bookmarks to my owner's computer because i want attention

Letters to my dog in heaven

Dear Co-Woofer, thanks for being my supportive four-legged "co-worker" and I wanted to tell you that I love...

You were my favorite co-woofer, right now I'd like to tell you...

Today you make me happy by remembering your favorite...

Today, you make me happy by...

Your favorite dog park was...

Favorite place to get your dog bath was...

Your rating in the Snuggles department was... ☆☆☆☆☆

Your favorite toy was...

The times you made me laughed so hard were...

I found it funny when you...

I loved it when you...

When you rolled over, you...

On our "break time" from work, you loved to...

At the dog parked, you hate...

At the dog parked, you like..

Some lessons I learned from knowing you are...

Your favorite place to be scratched was....

Favorite place to poop was....

Your favorite place to nap was...

Favorite TV show was...

My "support system" includes...

You loved to torture the...

Things I loved

- [ ] Squeaky toys
- [ ] Bath time
- [ ] The vet
- [ ] Being a good boy
- [ ] Playtime at the dog park
- [ ] Chewy toys
- [ ] Dog bones
- [ ] Treats for being cute
- [ ] Rubbing tail in owner's face
- [ ] Pawing for attention
- [ ] Sitting on the keyboard
- [ ] Kissing my owner's neck
- [ ] "Meetings" with my new manager at home
- [ ] Holding my owner's paws
- [ ] Receiving the max amount of petting i can get
- [ ] Personal lap warmer
- [ ] Gossiping with my co-woofer
- [ ] Trying to drink my owner's coffee while sitting on the laptop
- [ ] Accidentally adding bookmarks to my owner's computer because i want attention

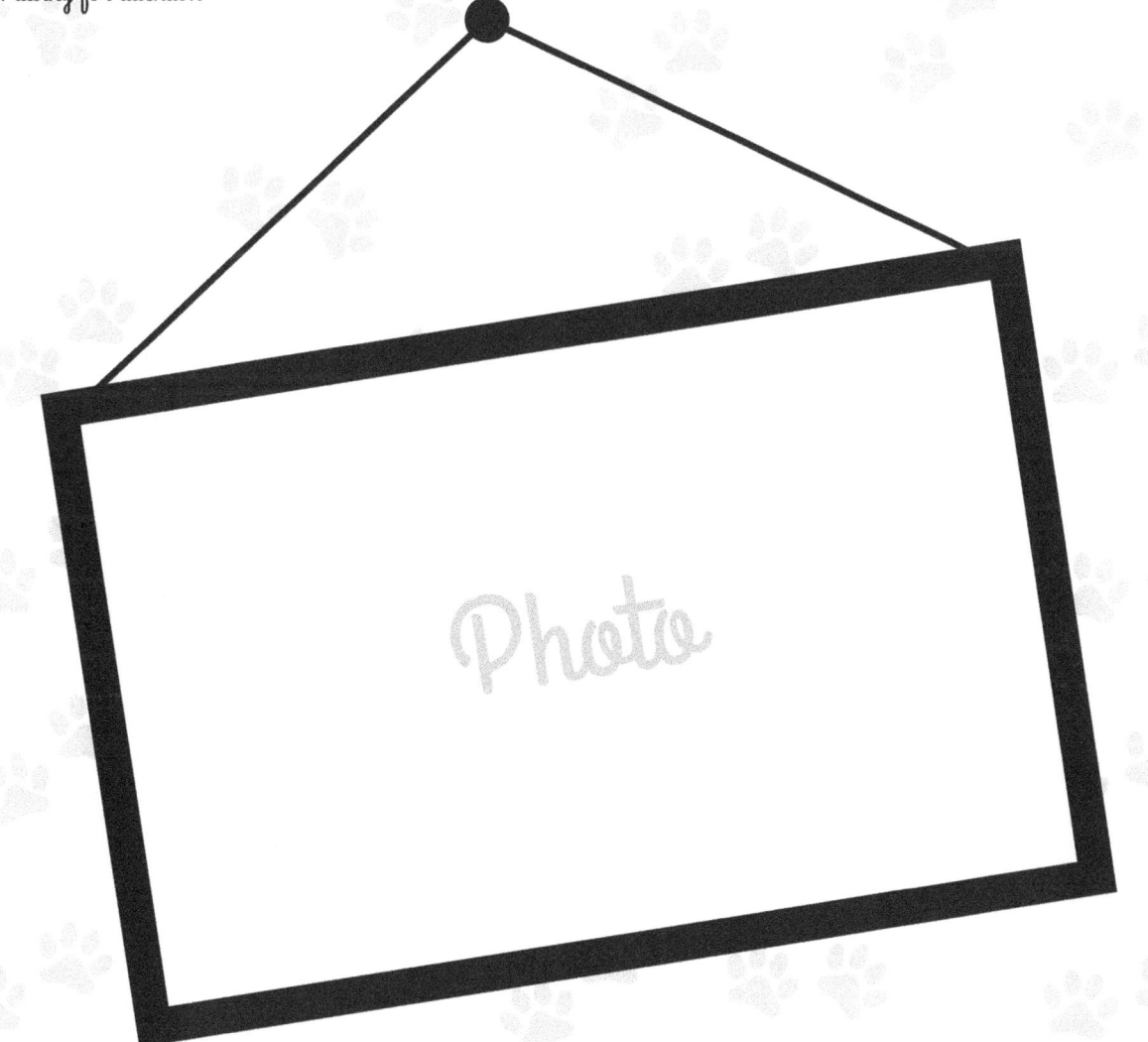

Letters to my dog in heaven

Dear Co-Woofer, thanks for being my supportive four-legged "co-worker" and I wanted to tell you that I love...

You were my favorite co-woofer, right now I'd like to tell you...

Today you make me happy by remembering your favorite...

Today, you make me happy by...

Your favorite dog park was...   Favorite place to get your dog bath was...   Your rating in the Snuggles department was...
☆ ☆ ☆ ☆ ☆

Your favorite toy was...   The times you made me laughed so hard were...

I found it funny when you...   I loved it when you...   When you rolled over, you...

On our "break time" from work, you loved to...

At the dog parked, you hate...

At the dog parked, you like..

Some lessons I learned from knowing you are...

Your favorite place to be scratched was....   Favorite place to poop was....   Your favorite place to nap was...

Favorite TV show was...   My "support system" includes...   You loved to torture the...

Things I loved

- [ ] Squeaky toys
- [ ] Bath time
- [ ] The vet
- [ ] Being a good boy
- [ ] Playtime at the dog park
- [ ] Chewy toys
- [ ] Dog bones
- [ ] Treats for being cute
- [ ] Rubbing tail in owner's face
- [ ] Pawing for attention
- [ ] Sitting on the keyboard
- [ ] Kissing my owner's neck
- [ ] "Meetings" with my new manager at home
- [ ] Holding my owner's paws
- [ ] Receiving the max amount of petting i can get
- [ ] Personal lap warmer
- [ ] Gossiping with my co-woofer
- [ ] Trying to drink my owner's coffee while sitting on the laptop
- [ ] Accidentally adding bookmarks to my owner's computer because i want attention

Letters to my dog in heaven

Dear Co-Woofer, thanks for being my supportive four-legged "co-worker" and I wanted to tell you that I love...

You were my favorite co-woofer, right now I'd like to tell you...

Today you make me happy by remembering your favorite...

Today, you make me happy by...

Your favorite dog park was...

Favorite place to get your dog bath was...

Your rating in the Snuggles department was...

☆ ☆ ☆ ☆ ☆

Your favorite toy was...

The times you made me laughed so hard were...

I found it funny when you...

I loved it when you...

When you rolled over, you...

On our "break time" from work, you loved to...

At the dog parked, you hate...

At the dog parked, you like..

Some lessons I learned from knowing you are...

Your favorite place to be scratched was....

Favorite place to poop was....

Your favorite place to nap was...

Favorite TV show was...

My "support system" includes...

You loved to torture the...

Things I loved

- [ ] Squeaky toys
- [ ] Bath time
- [ ] The vet
- [ ] Being a good boy
- [ ] Playtime at the dog park
- [ ] Chewy toys
- [ ] Dog bones
- [ ] Treats for being cute
- [ ] Rubbing tail in owner's face
- [ ] Pawing for attention
- [ ] Sitting on the keyboard
- [ ] Kissing my owner's neck
- [ ] "Meetings" with my new manager at home
- [ ] Holding my owner's paws
- [ ] Receiving the max amount of petting i can get
- [ ] Personal lap warmer
- [ ] Gossiping with my co-woofer
- [ ] Trying to drink my owner's coffee while sitting on the laptop
- [ ] Accidentally adding bookmarks to my owner's computer because i want attention

Letters to my dog in heaven

Dear Co-Woofer, thanks for being my supportive four-legged "co-worker" and I wanted to tell you that I love...

You were my favorite co-woofer, right now I'd like to tell you...

Today you make me happy by remembering your favorite...

Today, you make me happy by...

Your favorite dog park was...   Favorite place to get your dog bath was...   Your rating in the Snuggles department was... ☆☆☆☆☆

Your favorite toy was...   The times you made me laughed so hard were...

I found it funny when you...   I loved it when you...   When you rolled over, you...

On our "break time" from work, you loved to...

At the dog parked, you hate...

At the dog parked, you like..

Some lessons I learned from knowing you are...

Your favorite place to be scratched was....   Favorite place to poop was....   Your favorite place to nap was...

Favorite TV show was...   My "support system" includes...   You loved to torture the...

Things I loved

- [ ] Squeaky toys
- [ ] Bath time
- [ ] The vet
- [ ] Being a good boy
- [ ] Playtime at the dog park
- [ ] Chewy toys
- [ ] Dog bones
- [ ] Treats for being cute
- [ ] Rubbing tail in owner's face
- [ ] Pawing for attention
- [ ] Sitting on the keyboard
- [ ] Kissing my owner's neck
- [ ] "Meetings" with my new manager at home
- [ ] Holding my owner's paws
- [ ] Receiving the max amount of petting i can get
- [ ] Personal lap warmer
- [ ] Gossiping with my co-woofer
- [ ] Trying to drink my owner's coffee while sitting on the laptop
- [ ] Accidentally adding bookmarks to my owner's computer because i want attention

Letters to my dog in heaven

Dear Co-Woofer, thanks for being my supportive four-legged "co-worker" and I wanted to tell you that I love…

You were my favorite co-woofer, right now I'd like to tell you…

Today you make me happy by remembering your favorite…

Today, you make me happy by…

Your favorite dog park was…

Favorite place to get your dog bath was…

Your rating in the Snuggles department was…

☆ ☆ ☆ ☆ ☆

Your favorite toy was…

The times you made me laughed so hard were…

I found it funny when you…

I loved it when you…

When you rolled over, you…

On our "break time" from work, you loved to…

At the dog parked, you hate…

At the dog parked, you like..

Some lessons I learned from knowing you are…

Your favorite place to be scratched was….

Favorite place to poop was….

Your favorite place to nap was…

Favorite TV show was…

My "support system" includes…

You loved to torture the…

Things I loved

- ☐ Squeaky toys
- ☐ Bath time
- ☐ The vet
- ☐ Being a good boy
- ☐ Playtime at the dog park
- ☐ Chewy toys
- ☐ Dog bones
- ☐ Treats for being cute
- ☐ Rubbing tail in owner's face
- ☐ Pawing for attention
- ☐ Sitting on the keyboard
- ☐ Kissing my owner's neck
- ☐ "Meetings" with my new manager at home
- ☐ Holding my owner's paws
- ☐ Receiving the max amount of petting i can get
- ☐ Personal lap warmer
- ☐ Gossiping with my co-woofer
- ☐ Trying to drink my owner's coffee while sitting on the laptop
- ☐ Accidentally adding bookmarks to my owner's computer because i want attention

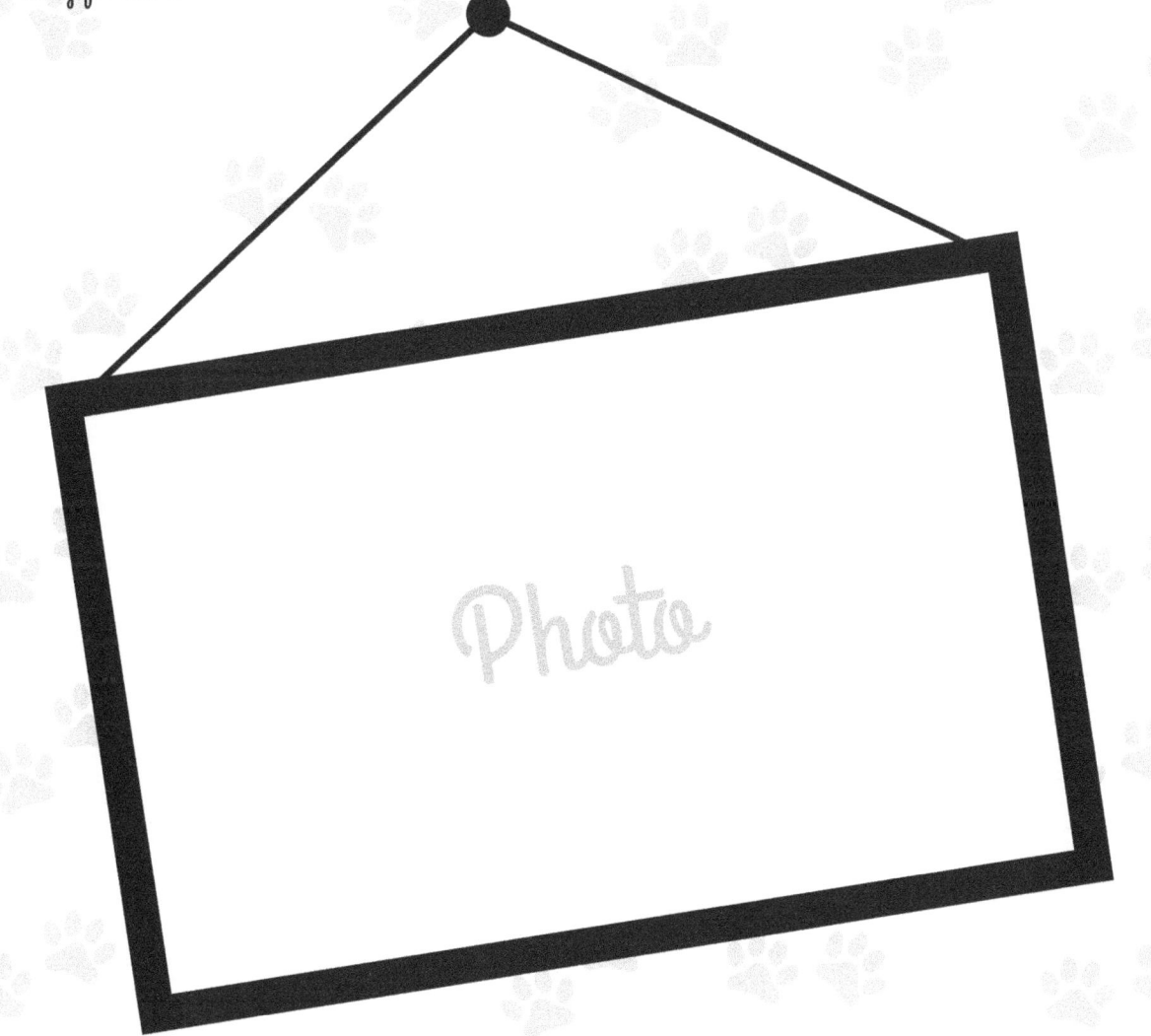

Letters to my dog in heaven

Dear Co-Woofer, thanks for being my supportive four-legged "co-worker" and I wanted to tell you that I love...

You were my favorite co-woofer, right now I'd like to tell you...

Today you make me happy by remembering your favorite...

Today, you make me happy by...

Your favorite dog park was...

Favorite place to get your dog bath was...

Your rating in the Snuggles department was...
☆ ☆ ☆ ☆ ☆

Your favorite toy was...

The times you made me laughed so hard were...

I found it funny when you...

I loved it when you...

When you rolled over, you...

On our "break time" from work, you loved to...

At the dog parked, you hate...

At the dog parked, you like..

Some lessons I learned from knowing you are...

Your favorite place to be scratched was....

Favorite place to poop was....

Your favorite place to nap was...

Favorite TV show was...

My "support system" includes...

You loved to torture the...

Things I loved

- ☐ Squeaky toys
- ☐ Bath time
- ☐ The vet
- ☐ Being a good boy
- ☐ Playtime at the dog park
- ☐ Chewy toys
- ☐ Dog bones
- ☐ Treats for being cute
- ☐ Rubbing tail in owner's face
- ☐ Pawing for attention
- ☐ Sitting on the keyboard
- ☐ Kissing my owner's neck
- ☐ "Meetings" with my new manager at home
- ☐ Holding my owner's paws
- ☐ Receiving the max amount of petting i can get
- ☐ Personal lap warmer
- ☐ Gossiping with my co-woofer
- ☐ Trying to drink my owner's coffee while sitting on the laptop
- ☐ Accidentally adding bookmarks to my owner's computer because i want attention

Letters to my dog in heaven

Dear Co-Woofer, thanks for being my supportive four-legged "co-worker" and I wanted to tell you that I love...

You were my favorite co-woofer, right now I'd like to tell you...

Today you make me happy by remembering your favorite...

Today, you make me happy by...

Your favorite dog park was...

Favorite place to get your dog bath was...

Your rating in the Snuggles department was... ☆ ☆ ☆ ☆ ☆

Your favorite toy was...

The times you made me laughed so hard were...

I found it funny when you...

I loved it when you...

When you rolled over, you...

On our "break time" from work, you loved to...

At the dog parked, you hate...

At the dog parked, you like..

Some lessons I learned from knowing you are...

Your favorite place to be scratched was....

Favorite place to poop was....

Your favorite place to nap was...

Favorite TV show was...

My "support system" includes...

You loved to torture the...

Things I loved

- [ ] Squeaky toys
- [ ] Bath time
- [ ] The vet
- [ ] Being a good boy
- [ ] Playtime at the dog park
- [ ] Chewy toys
- [ ] Dog bones
- [ ] Treats for being cute
- [ ] Rubbing tail in owner's face
- [ ] Pawing for attention
- [ ] Sitting on the keyboard
- [ ] Kissing my owner's neck
- [ ] "Meetings" with my new manager at home
- [ ] Holding my owner's paws
- [ ] Receiving the max amount of petting i can get
- [ ] Personal lap warmer
- [ ] Gossiping with my co-woofer
- [ ] Trying to drink my owner's coffee while sitting on the laptop
- [ ] Accidentally adding bookmarks to my owner's computer because i want attention

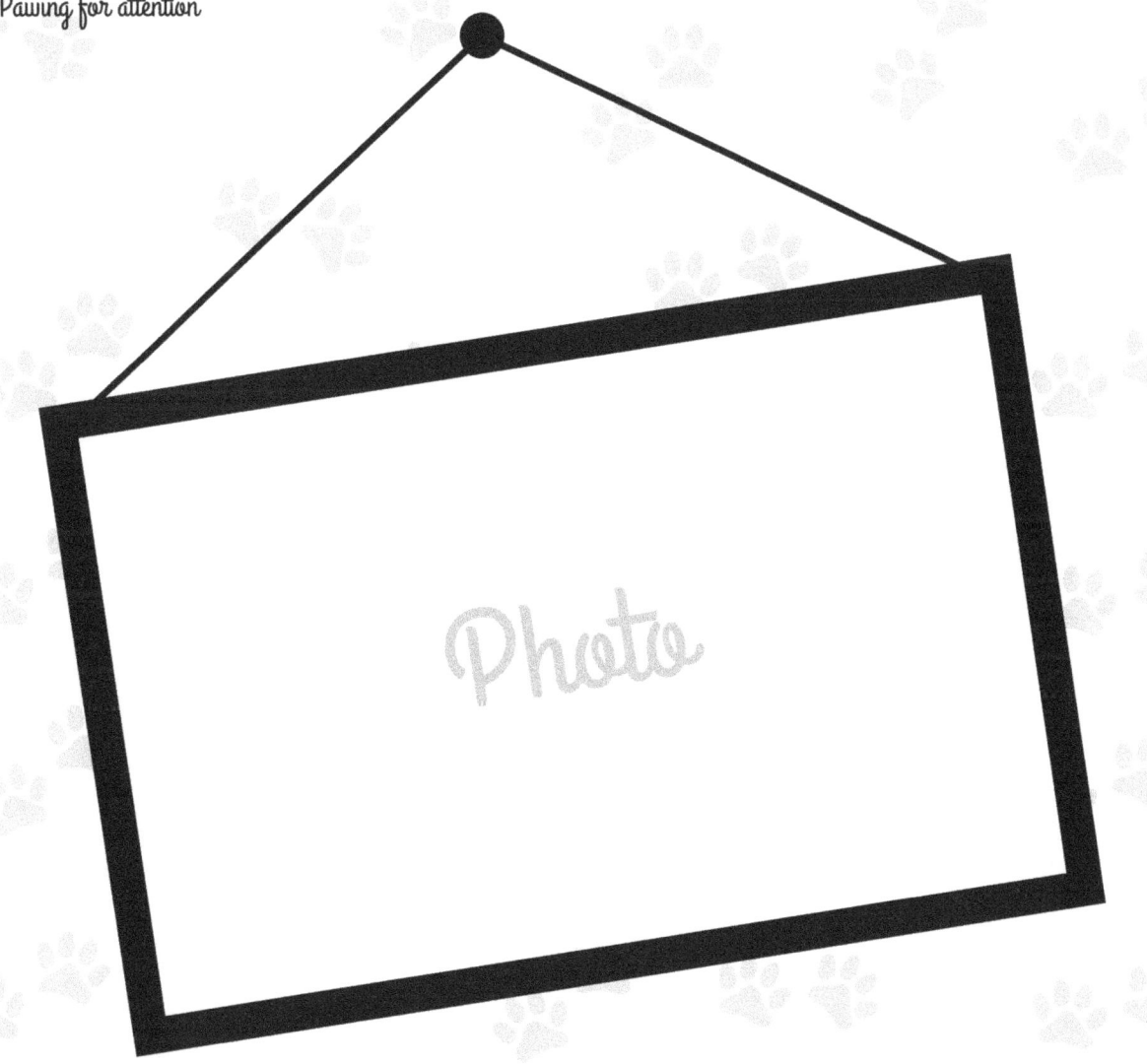

Letters to my dog in heaven

Dear Co-Woofer, thanks for being my supportive four-legged "co-worker" and I wanted to tell you that I love...

You were my favorite co-woofer, right now I'd like to tell you...

Today you make me happy by remembering your favorite...

Today, you make me happy by...

Your favorite dog park was... Favorite place to get your dog bath was... Your rating in the Snuggles department was...

☆ ☆ ☆ ☆ ☆

Your favorite toy was... The times you made me laughed so hard were...

I found it funny when you... I loved it when you... When you rolled over, you...

On our "break time" from work, you loved to...

At the dog parked, you hate...

At the dog parked, you like..

Some lessons I learned from knowing you are...

Your favorite place to be scratched was.... Favorite place to poop was.... Your favorite place to nap was...

Favorite TV show was... My "support system" includes... You loved to torture the...

Things I loved

- [ ] Squeaky toys
- [ ] Bath time
- [ ] The vet
- [ ] Being a good boy
- [ ] Playtime at the dog park
- [ ] Chewy toys
- [ ] Dog bones
- [ ] Treats for being cute
- [ ] Rubbing tail in owner's face
- [ ] Pawing for attention
- [ ] Sitting on the keyboard
- [ ] Kissing my owner's neck
- [ ] "Meetings" with my new manager at home
- [ ] Holding my owner's paws
- [ ] Receiving the max amount of petting i can get
- [ ] Personal lap warmer
- [ ] Gossiping with my co-woofer
- [ ] Trying to drink my owner's coffee while sitting on the laptop
- [ ] Accidentally adding bookmarks to my owner's computer because i want attention

Letters to my dog in heaven

Dear Co-Woofer, thanks for being my supportive four-legged "co-worker" and I wanted to tell you that I love...

You were my favorite co-woofer, right now I'd like to tell you...

Today you make me happy by remembering your favorite...

Today, you make me happy by...

Your favorite dog park was...

Favorite place to get your dog bath was...

Your rating in the Snuggles department was...
☆ ☆ ☆ ☆ ☆

Your favorite toy was...

The times you made me laughed so hard were...

I found it funny when you...

I loved it when you...

When you rolled over, you...

On our "break time" from work, you loved to...

At the dog parked, you hate...

At the dog parked, you like..

Some lessons I learned from knowing you are...

Your favorite place to be scratched was....

Favorite place to poop was....

Your favorite place to nap was...

Favorite TV show was...

My "support system" includes...

You loved to torture the...

Things I loved

- [ ] Squeaky toys
- [ ] Bath time
- [ ] The vet
- [ ] Being a good boy
- [ ] Playtime at the dog park
- [ ] Chewy toys
- [ ] Dog bones
- [ ] Treats for being cute
- [ ] Rubbing tail in owner's face
- [ ] Pawing for attention
- [ ] Sitting on the keyboard
- [ ] Kissing my owner's neck
- [ ] "Meetings" with my new manager at home
- [ ] Holding my owner's paws
- [ ] Receiving the max amount of petting i can get
- [ ] Personal lap warmer
- [ ] Gossiping with my co-woofer
- [ ] Trying to drink my owner's coffee while sitting on the laptop
- [ ] Accidentally adding bookmarks to my owner's computer because i want attention

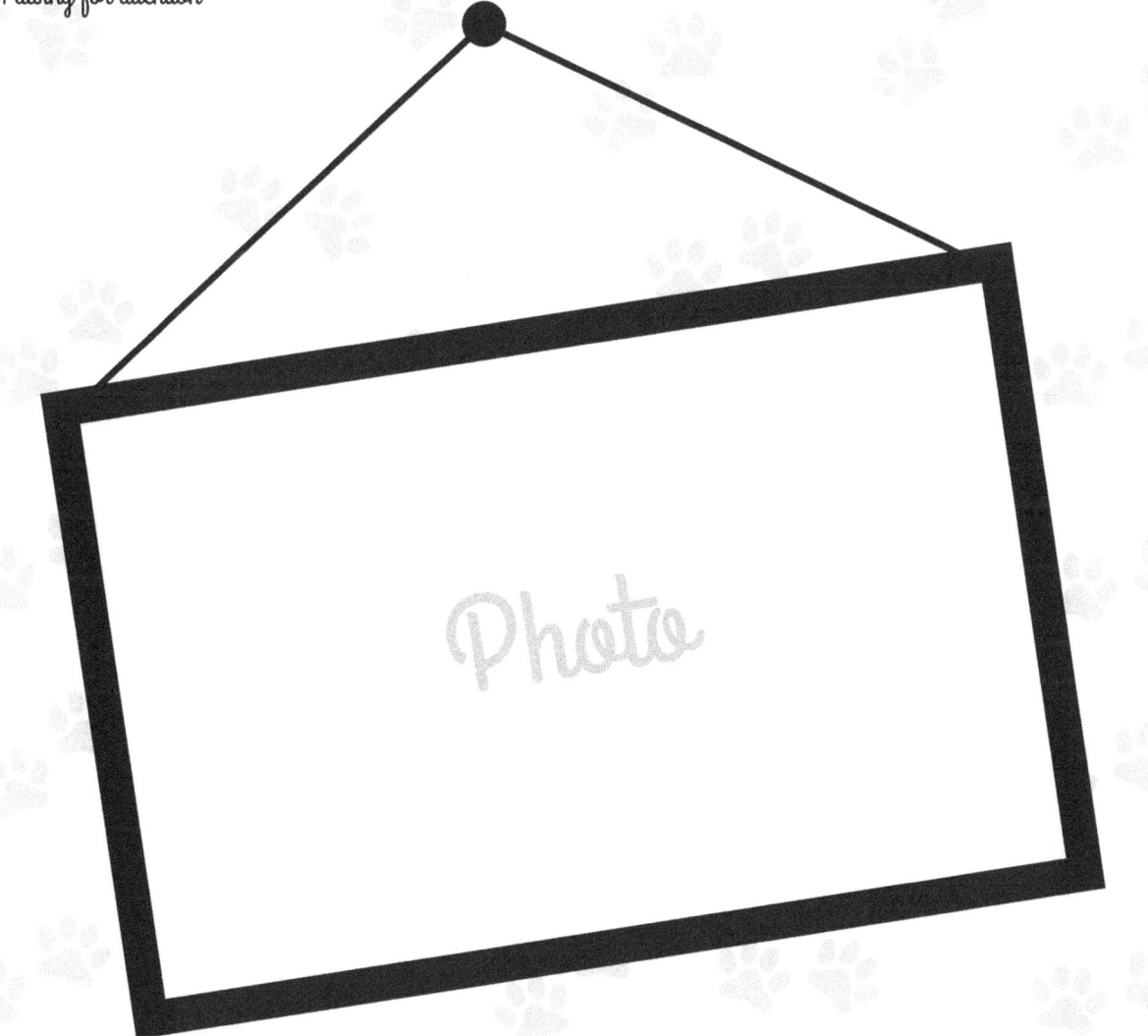

Letters to my dog in heaven

Dear Co-Woofer, thanks for being my supportive four-legged "co-worker" and I wanted to tell you that I love...

You were my favorite co-woofer, right now I'd like to tell you...

Today you make me happy by remembering your favorite...

Today, you make me happy by...

Your favorite dog park was...

Favorite place to get your dog bath was...

Your rating in the Snuggles department was...
☆ ☆ ☆ ☆ ☆

Your favorite toy was...

The times you made me laughed so hard were...

I found it funny when you...

I loved it when you...

When you rolled over, you...

On our "break time" from work, you loved to...

At the dog parked, you hate...

At the dog parked, you like..

Some lessons I learned from knowing you are...

Your favorite place to be scratched was....

Favorite place to poop was....

Your favorite place to nap was...

Favorite TV show was...

My "support system" includes...

You loved to torture the...

Things I loved

- [ ] Squeaky toys
- [ ] Bath time
- [ ] The vet
- [ ] Being a good boy
- [ ] Playtime at the dog park
- [ ] Chewy toys
- [ ] Dog bones
- [ ] Treats for being cute
- [ ] Rubbing tail in owner's face
- [ ] Pawing for attention
- [ ] Sitting on the keyboard
- [ ] Kissing my owner's neck
- [ ] "Meetings" with my new manager at home
- [ ] Holding my owner's paws
- [ ] Receiving the max amount of petting i can get
- [ ] Personal lap warmer
- [ ] Gossiping with my co-woofer
- [ ] Trying to drink my owner's coffee while sitting on the laptop
- [ ] Accidentally adding bookmarks to my owner's computer because i want attention

Letters to my dog in heaven

Dear Co-Woofer, thanks for being my supportive four-legged "co-worker" and I wanted to tell you that I love...

You were my favorite co-woofer, right now I'd like to tell you...

Today you make me happy by remembering your favorite...

Today, you make me happy by...

Your favorite dog park was...   Favorite place to get your dog bath was...   Your rating in the Snuggles department was.. ☆☆☆☆☆

Your favorite toy was...   The times you made me laughed so hard were...

I found it funny when you...   I loved it when you...   When you rolled over, you...

On our "break time" from work, you loved to...

At the dog parked, you hate...

At the dog parked, you like..

Some lessons I learned from knowing you are...

Your favorite place to be scratched was....   Favorite place to poop was....   Your favorite place to nap was...

Favorite TV show was...   My "support system" includes...   You loved to torture the...

Things I loved

- [ ] Squeaky toys
- [ ] Bath time
- [ ] The vet
- [ ] Being a good boy
- [ ] Playtime at the dog park
- [ ] Chewy toys
- [ ] Dog bones
- [ ] Treats for being cute
- [ ] Rubbing tail in owner's face
- [ ] Pawing for attention
- [ ] Sitting on the keyboard
- [ ] Kissing my owner's neck
- [ ] "Meetings" with my new manager at home
- [ ] Holding my owner's paws
- [ ] Receiving the max amount of petting i can get
- [ ] Personal lap warmer
- [ ] Gossiping with my co-woofer
- [ ] Trying to drink my owner's coffee while sitting on the laptop
- [ ] Accidentally adding bookmarks to my owner's computer because i want attention

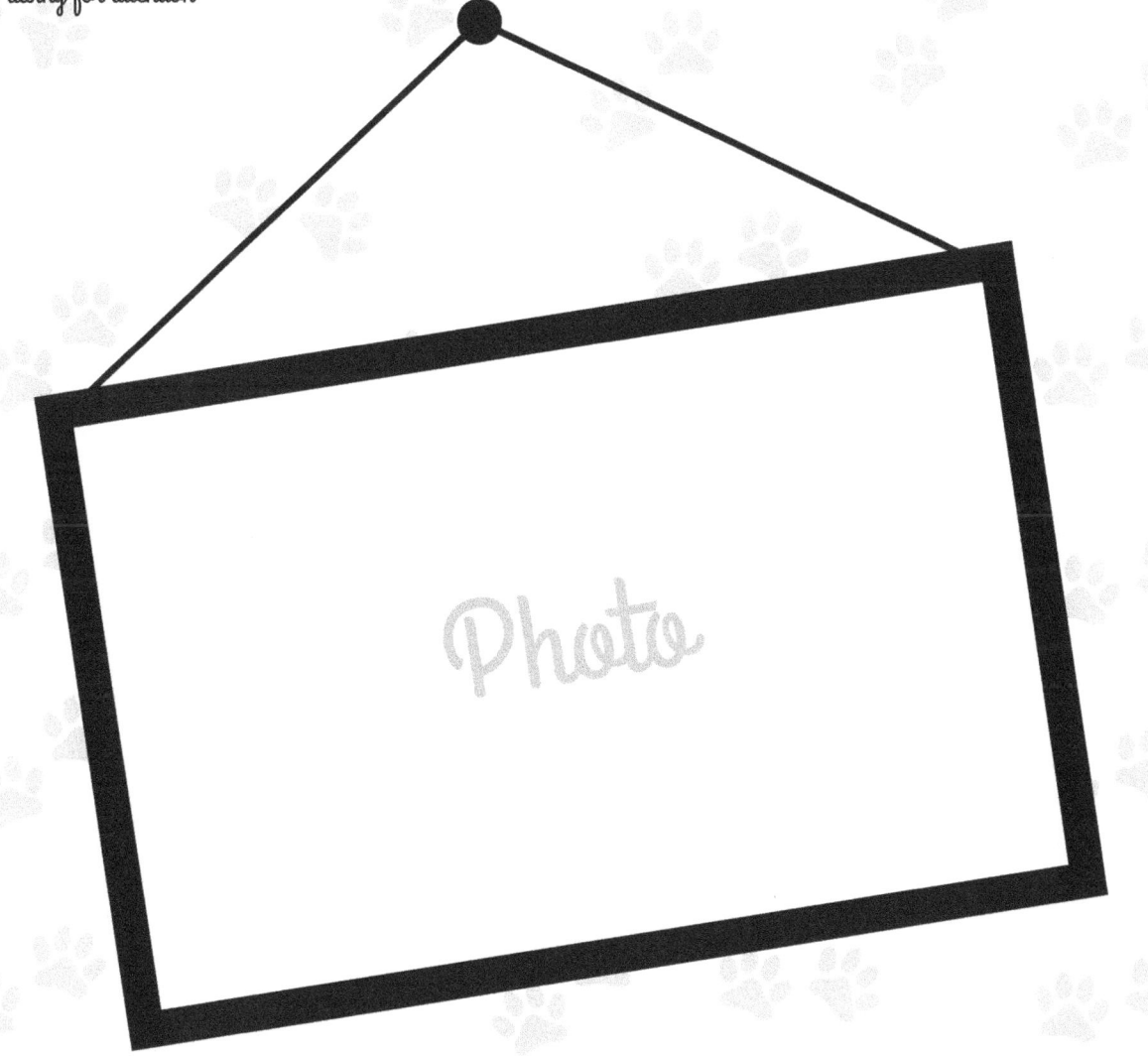

Letters to my dog in heaven

Dear Co-Woofer, thanks for being my supportive four-legged "co-worker" and I wanted to tell you that I love...

You were my favorite co-woofer, right now I'd like to tell you...

Today you make me happy by remembering your favorite...

Today, you make me happy by...

Your favorite dog park was...   Favorite place to get your dog bath was...   Your rating in the Snuggles department was...
☆ ☆ ☆ ☆ ☆

Your favorite toy was...   The times you made me laughed so hard were...

I found it funny when you...   I loved it when you...   When you rolled over, you...

On our "break time" from work, you loved to...

At the dog parked, you hate...

At the dog parked, you like..

Some lessons I learned from knowing you are...

Your favorite place to be scratched was....   Favorite place to poop was....   Your favorite place to nap was...

Favorite TV show was...   My "support system" includes...   You loved to torture the...

Things I loved

- ☐ Squeaky toys
- ☐ Bath time
- ☐ The vet
- ☐ Being a good boy
- ☐ Playtime at the dog park
- ☐ Chewy toys
- ☐ Dog bones
- ☐ Treats for being cute
- ☐ Rubbing tail in owner's face
- ☐ Pawing for attention
- ☐ Sitting on the keyboard
- ☐ Kissing my owner's neck
- ☐ "Meetings" with my new manager at home
- ☐ Holding my owner's paws
- ☐ Receiving the max amount of petting i can get
- ☐ Personal lap warmer
- ☐ Gossiping with my co-woofer
- ☐ Trying to drink my owner's coffee while sitting on the laptop
- ☐ Accidentally adding bookmarks to my owner's computer because i want attention

Letters to my dog in heaven

Dear Co-Woofer, thanks for being my supportive four-legged "co-worker" and I wanted to tell you that I love...

You were my favorite co-woofer, right now I'd like to tell you...

Today you make me happy by remembering your favorite...

Today, you make me happy by...

Your favorite dog park was...   Favorite place to get your dog bath was...   Your rating in the Snuggles department was... ☆☆☆☆☆

Your favorite toy was...   The times you made me laughed so hard were...

I found it funny when you...   I loved it when you...   When you rolled over, you...

On our "break time" from work, you loved to...

At the dog parked, you hate...

At the dog parked, you like..

Some lessons I learned from knowing you are...

Your favorite place to be scratched was....   Favorite place to poop was....   Your favorite place to nap was...

Favorite TV show was...   My "support system" includes...   You loved to torture the...

Things I loved

- [ ] Squeaky toys
- [ ] Bath time
- [ ] The vet
- [ ] Being a good boy
- [ ] Playtime at the dog park
- [ ] Chewy toys
- [ ] Dog bones
- [ ] Treats for being cute
- [ ] Rubbing tail in owner's face
- [ ] Pawing for attention
- [ ] Sitting on the keyboard
- [ ] Kissing my owner's neck
- [ ] "Meetings" with my new manager at home
- [ ] Holding my owner's paws
- [ ] Receiving the max amount of petting i can get
- [ ] Personal lap warmer
- [ ] Gossiping with my co-woofer
- [ ] Trying to drink my owner's coffee while sitting on the laptop
- [ ] Accidentally adding bookmarks to my owner's computer because i want attention

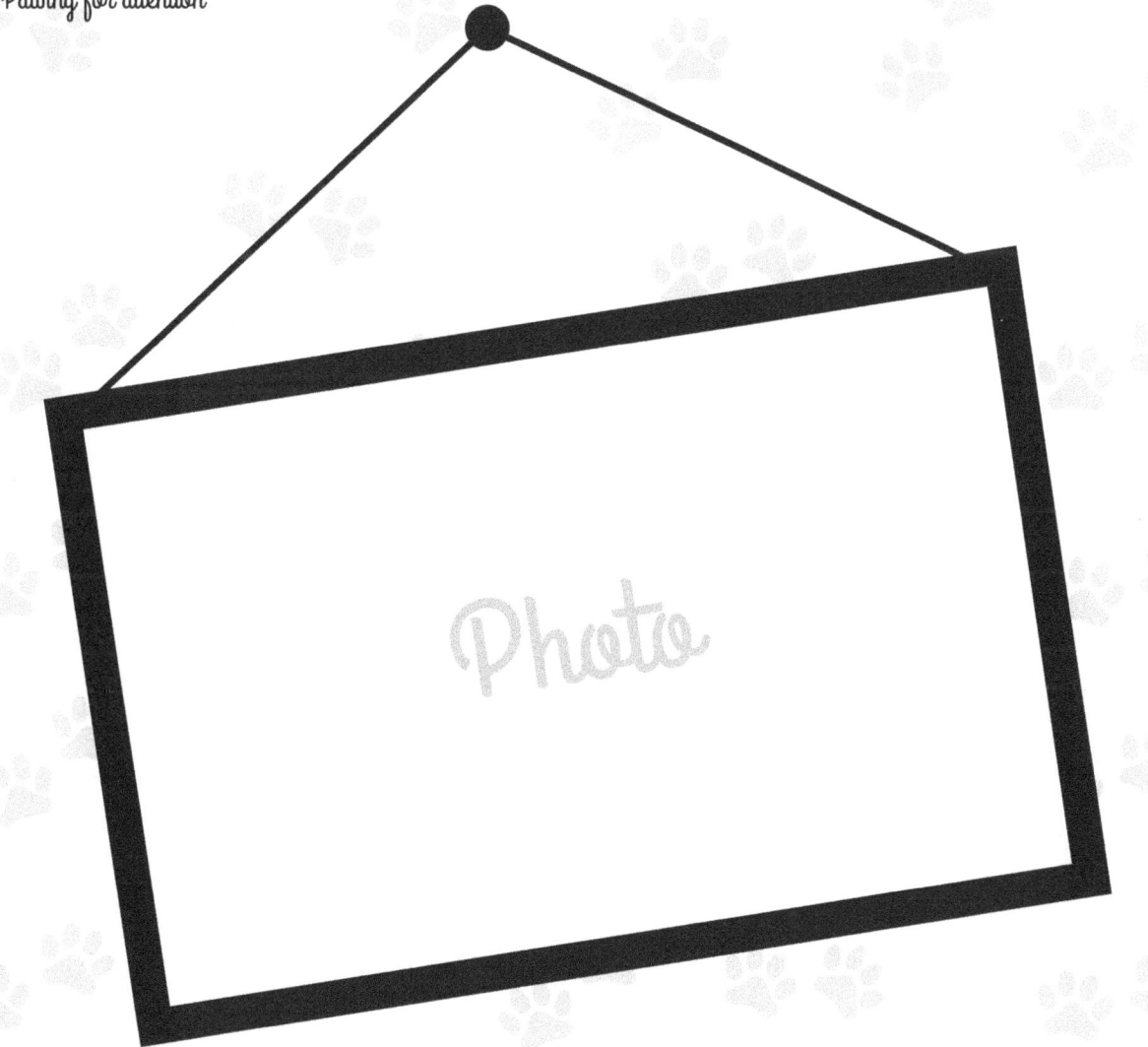

Letters to my dog in heaven

Dear Co-Woofer, thanks for being my supportive four-legged "co-worker" and I wanted to tell you that I love...

You were my favorite co-woofer, right now I'd like to tell you...

Today you make me happy by remembering your favorite...

Today, you make me happy by...

Your favorite dog park was...   Favorite place to get your dog bath was...   Your rating in the Snuggles department was...
☆ ☆ ☆ ☆ ☆

Your favorite toy was...   The times you made me laughed so hard were...

I found it funny when you...   I loved it when you...   When you rolled over, you...

On our "break time" from work, you loved to...

At the dog parked, you hate...

At the dog parked, you like..

Some lessons I learned from knowing you are...

Your favorite place to be scratched was....   Favorite place to poop was....   Your favorite place to nap was...

Favorite TV show was...   My "support system" includes...   You loved to torture the...

Things I loved

- [ ] Squeaky toys
- [ ] Bath time
- [ ] The vet
- [ ] Being a good boy
- [ ] Playtime at the dog park
- [ ] Chewy toys
- [ ] Dog bones
- [ ] Treats for being cute
- [ ] Rubbing tail in owner's face
- [ ] Pawing for attention
- [ ] Sitting on the keyboard
- [ ] Kissing my owner's neck
- [ ] "Meetings" with my new manager at home
- [ ] Holding my owner's paws
- [ ] Receiving the max amount of petting i can get
- [ ] Personal lap warmer
- [ ] Gossiping with my co-woofer
- [ ] Trying to drink my owner's coffee while sitting on the laptop
- [ ] Accidentally adding bookmarks to my owner's computer because i want attention

Letters to my dog in heaven

Dear Co-Woofer, thanks for being my supportive four-legged "co-worker" and I wanted to tell you that I love...

You were my favorite co-woofer, right now I'd like to tell you...

Today you make me happy by remembering your favorite...

Today, you make me happy by...

Your favorite dog park was...

Favorite place to get your dog bath was...

Your rating in the Snuggles department was...

☆ ☆ ☆ ☆ ☆

Your favorite toy was...

The times you made me laughed so hard were...

I found it funny when you...

I loved it when you...

When you rolled over, you...

On our "break time" from work, you loved to...

At the dog parked, you hate...

At the dog parked, you like..

Some lessons I learned from knowing you are...

Your favorite place to be scratched was....

Favorite place to poop was....

Your favorite place to nap was...

Favorite TV show was...

My "support system" includes...

You loved to torture the...

Things I loved

- [ ] Squeaky toys
- [ ] Bath time
- [ ] The vet
- [ ] Being a good boy
- [ ] Playtime at the dog park
- [ ] Chewy toys
- [ ] Dog bones
- [ ] Treats for being cute
- [ ] Rubbing tail in owner's face
- [ ] Pawing for attention
- [ ] Sitting on the keyboard
- [ ] Kissing my owner's neck
- [ ] "Meetings" with my new manager at home
- [ ] Holding my owner's paws
- [ ] Receiving the max amount of petting i can get
- [ ] Personal lap warmer
- [ ] Gossiping with my co-woofer
- [ ] Trying to drink my owner's coffee while sitting on the laptop
- [ ] Accidentally adding bookmarks to my owner's computer because i want attention

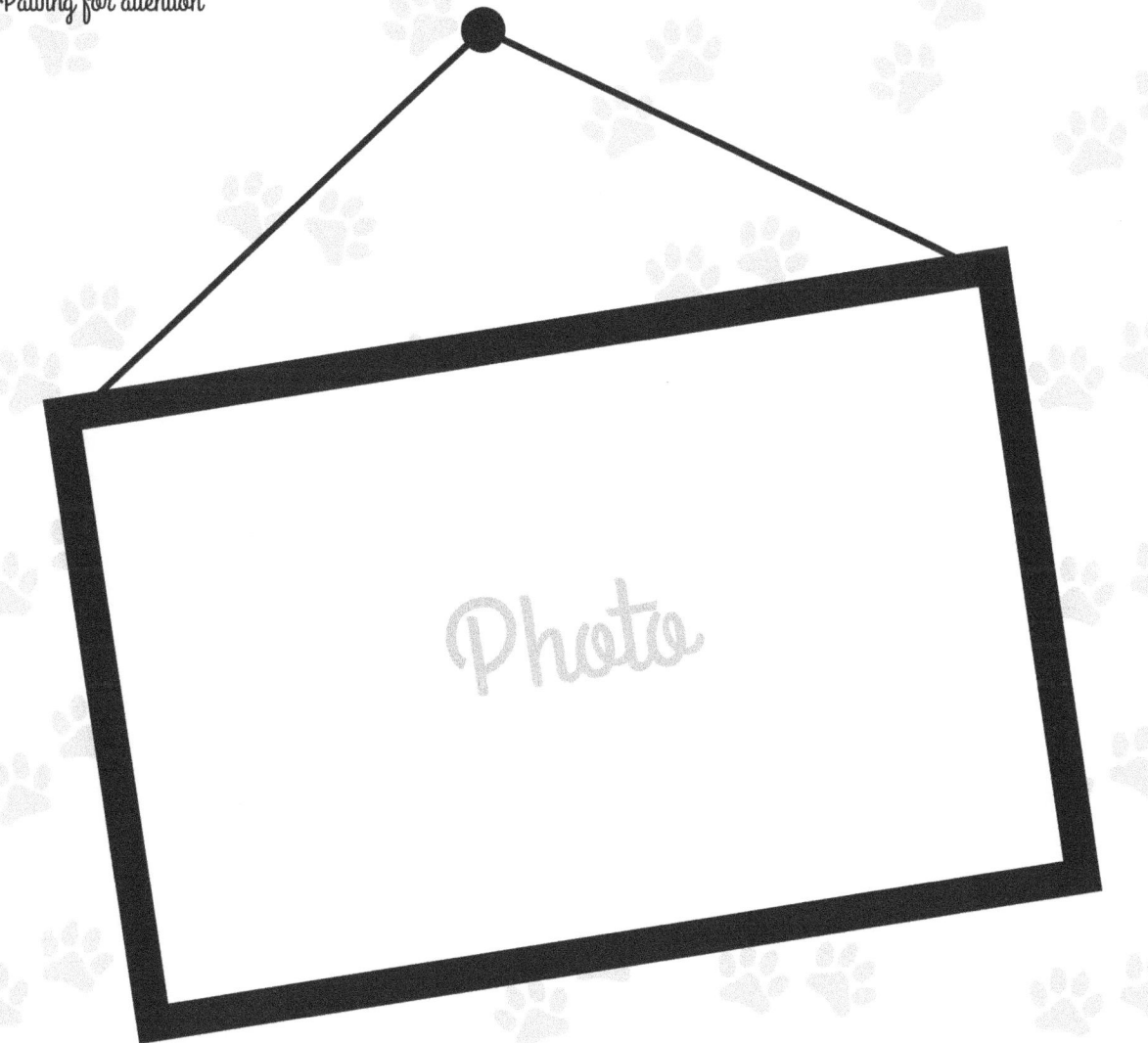

Letters to my dog in heaven

Dear Co-Woofer, thanks for being my supportive four-legged "co-worker" and I wanted to tell you that I love...

You were my favorite co-woofer, right now I'd like to tell you...

Today you make me happy by remembering your favorite...

Today, you make me happy by...

Your favorite dog park was...

Favorite place to get your dog bath was...

Your rating in the Snuggles department was...
☆ ☆ ☆ ☆ ☆

Your favorite toy was...

The times you made me laughed so hard were...

I found it funny when you...

I loved it when you...

When you rolled over, you...

On our "break time" from work, you loved to...

At the dog parked, you hate...

At the dog parked, you like..

Some lessons I learned from knowing you are...

Your favorite place to be scratched was....

Favorite place to poop was....

Your favorite place to nap was...

Favorite TV show was...

My "support system" includes...

You loved to torture the...

Things I loved

- ☐ Squeaky toys
- ☐ Bath time
- ☐ The vet
- ☐ Being a good boy
- ☐ Playtime at the dog park
- ☐ Chewy toys
- ☐ Dog bones
- ☐ Treats for being cute
- ☐ Rubbing tail in owner's face
- ☐ Pawing for attention
- ☐ Sitting on the keyboard
- ☐ Kissing my owner's neck
- ☐ "Meetings" with my new manager at home
- ☐ Holding my owner's paws
- ☐ Receiving the max amount of petting i can get
- ☐ Personal lap warmer
- ☐ Gossiping with my co-woofer
- ☐ Trying to drink my owner's coffee while sitting on the laptop
- ☐ Accidentally adding bookmarks to my owner's computer because i want attention

Photo

Letters to my dog in heaven

Dear Co-Woofer, thanks for being my supportive four-legged "co-worker" and I wanted to tell you that I love...

You were my favorite co-woofer, right now I'd like to tell you...

Today you make me happy by remembering your favorite...

Today, you make me happy by...

Your favorite dog park was... | Favorite place to get your dog bath was... | Your rating in the Snuggles department was... ☆☆☆☆☆

Your favorite toy was... | The times you made me laughed so hard were...

I found it funny when you... | I loved it when you... | When you rolled over, you...

On our "break time" from work, you loved to...

At the dog parked, you hate...

At the dog parked, you like..

Some lessons I learned from knowing you are...

Your favorite place to be scratched was.... | Favorite place to poop was.... | Your favorite place to nap was...

Favorite TV show was... | My "support system" includes... | You loved to torture the...

Things I loved

- [ ] Squeaky toys
- [ ] Bath time
- [ ] The vet
- [ ] Being a good boy
- [ ] Playtime at the dog park
- [ ] Chewy toys
- [ ] Dog bones
- [ ] Treats for being cute
- [ ] Rubbing tail in owner's face
- [ ] Pawing for attention
- [ ] Sitting on the keyboard
- [ ] Kissing my owner's neck
- [ ] "Meetings" with my new manager at home
- [ ] Holding my owner's paws
- [ ] Receiving the max amount of petting i can get
- [ ] Personal lap warmer
- [ ] Gossiping with my co-woofer
- [ ] Trying to drink my owner's coffee while sitting on the laptop
- [ ] Accidentally adding bookmarks to my owner's computer because i want attention

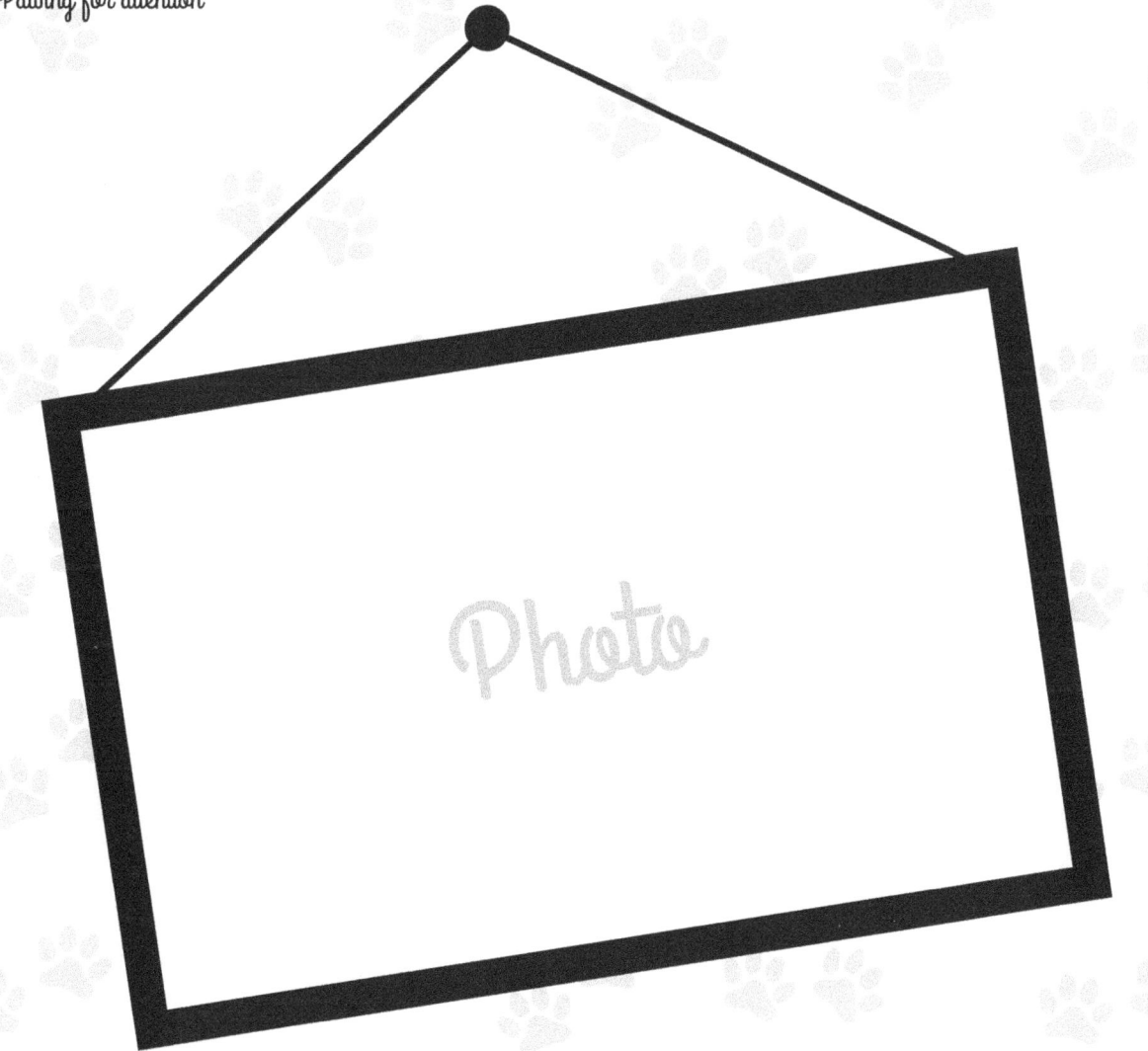

Letters to my dog in heaven

Dear Co-Woofer, thanks for being my supportive four-legged "co-worker" and I wanted to tell you that I love...

You were my favorite co-woofer, right now I'd like to tell you...

Today you make me happy by remembering your favorite...

Today, you make me happy by...

Your favorite dog park was...

Favorite place to get your dog bath was...

Your rating in the Snuggles department was... ☆☆☆☆☆

Your favorite toy was...

The times you made me laughed so hard were...

I found it funny when you...

I loved it when you...

When you rolled over, you...

On our "break time" from work, you loved to...

At the dog parked, you hate...

At the dog parked, you like..

Some lessons I learned from knowing you are...

Your favorite place to be scratched was....

Favorite place to poop was....

Your favorite place to nap was...

Favorite TV show was...

My "support system" includes...

You loved to torture the...

Things I loved

- ☐ Squeaky toys
- ☐ Bath time
- ☐ The vet
- ☐ Being a good boy
- ☐ Playtime at the dog park
- ☐ Chewy toys
- ☐ Dog bones
- ☐ Treats for being cute
- ☐ Rubbing tail in owner's face
- ☐ Pawing for attention
- ☐ Sitting on the keyboard
- ☐ Kissing my owner's neck
- ☐ "Meetings" with my new manager at home
- ☐ Holding my owner's paws
- ☐ Receiving the max amount of petting i can get
- ☐ Personal lap warmer
- ☐ Gossiping with my co-woofer
- ☐ Trying to drink my owner's coffee while sitting on the laptop
- ☐ Accidentally adding bookmarks to my owner's computer because i want attention

Letters to my dog in heaven

Dear Co-Woofer, thanks for being my supportive four-legged "co-worker" and I wanted to tell you that I love...

You were my favorite co-woofer, right now I'd like to tell you...

Today you make me happy by remembering your favorite...

Today, you make me happy by...

Your favorite dog park was...

Favorite place to get your dog bath was...

Your rating in the Snuggles department was... ☆☆☆☆☆

Your favorite toy was...

The times you made me laughed so hard were...

I found it funny when you...

I loved it when you...

When you rolled over, you...

On our "break time" from work, you loved to...

At the dog parked, you hate...

At the dog parked, you like..

Some lessons I learned from knowing you are...

Your favorite place to be scratched was....

Favorite place to poop was....

Your favorite place to nap was...

Favorite TV show was...

My "support system" includes...

You loved to torture the...

Things I loved

- [ ] Squeaky toys
- [ ] Bath time
- [ ] The vet
- [ ] Being a good boy
- [ ] Playtime at the dog park
- [ ] Chewy toys
- [ ] Dog bones
- [ ] Treats for being cute
- [ ] Rubbing tail in owner's face
- [ ] Pawing for attention
- [ ] Sitting on the keyboard
- [ ] Kissing my owner's neck
- [ ] "Meetings" with my new manager at home
- [ ] Holding my owner's paws
- [ ] Receiving the max amount of petting i can get
- [ ] Personal lap warmer
- [ ] Gossiping with my co-woofer
- [ ] Trying to drink my owner's coffee while sitting on the laptop
- [ ] Accidentally adding bookmarks to my owner's computer because i want attention

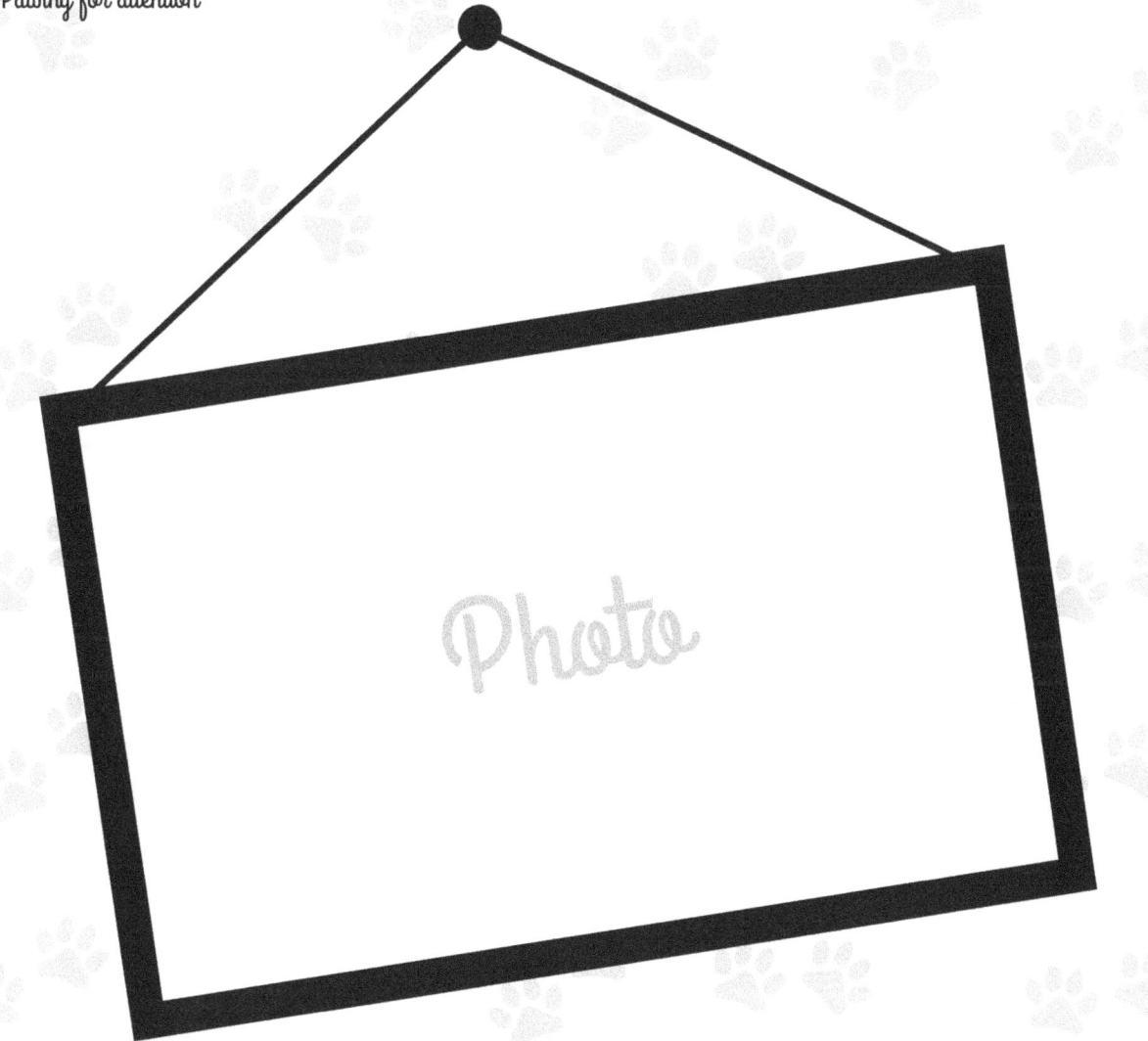

Letters to my dog in heaven

Dear Co-Woofer, thanks for being my supportive four-legged "co-worker" and I wanted to tell you that I love...

You were my favorite co-woofer, right now I'd like to tell you...

Today you make me happy by remembering your favorite...

Today, you make me happy by...

Your favorite dog park was...

Favorite place to get your dog bath was...

Your rating in the Snuggles department was... ☆☆☆☆☆

Your favorite toy was...

The times you made me laughed so hard were...

I found it funny when you...

I loved it when you...

When you rolled over, you...

On our "break time" from work, you loved to...

At the dog parked, you hate...

At the dog parked, you like..

Some lessons I learned from knowing you are...

Your favorite place to be scratched was....

Favorite place to poop was....

Your favorite place to nap was...

Favorite TV show was...

My "support system" includes...

You loved to torture the...

Things I loved

- [ ] Squeaky toys
- [ ] Bath time
- [ ] The vet
- [ ] Being a good boy
- [ ] Playtime at the dog park
- [ ] Chewy toys
- [ ] Dog bones
- [ ] Treats for being cute
- [ ] Rubbing tail in owner's face
- [ ] Pawing for attention
- [ ] Sitting on the keyboard
- [ ] Kissing my owner's neck
- [ ] "Meetings" with my new manager at home
- [ ] Holding my owner's paws
- [ ] Receiving the max amount of petting i can get
- [ ] Personal lap warmer
- [ ] Gossiping with my co-woofer
- [ ] Trying to drink my owner's coffee while sitting on the laptop
- [ ] Accidentally adding bookmarks to my owner's computer because i want attention

Photo

Letters to my dog in heaven

Dear Co-Woofer, thanks for being my supportive four-legged "co-worker" and I wanted to tell you that I love...

You were my favorite co-woofer, right now I'd like to tell you...

Today you make me happy by remembering your favorite...

Today, you make me happy by...

Your favorite dog park was...

Favorite place to get your dog bath was...

Your rating in the Snuggles department was... ☆☆☆☆☆

Your favorite toy was...

The times you made me laughed so hard were...

I found it funny when you...

I loved it when you...

When you rolled over, you...

On our "break time" from work, you loved to...

At the dog parked, you hate...

At the dog parked, you like..

Some lessons I learned from knowing you are...

Your favorite place to be scratched was....

Favorite place to poop was....

Your favorite place to nap was...

Favorite TV show was...

My "support system" includes...

You loved to torture the...

Things I loved

- [ ] Squeaky toys
- [ ] Bath time
- [ ] The vet
- [ ] Being a good boy
- [ ] Playtime at the dog park
- [ ] Chewy toys
- [ ] Dog bones
- [ ] Treats for being cute
- [ ] Rubbing tail in owner's face
- [ ] Pawing for attention
- [ ] Sitting on the keyboard
- [ ] Kissing my owner's neck
- [ ] "Meetings" with my new manager at home
- [ ] Holding my owner's paws
- [ ] Receiving the max amount of petting i can get
- [ ] Personal lap warmer
- [ ] Gossiping with my co-woofer
- [ ] Trying to drink my owner's coffee while sitting on the laptop
- [ ] Accidentally adding bookmarks to my owner's computer because i want attention

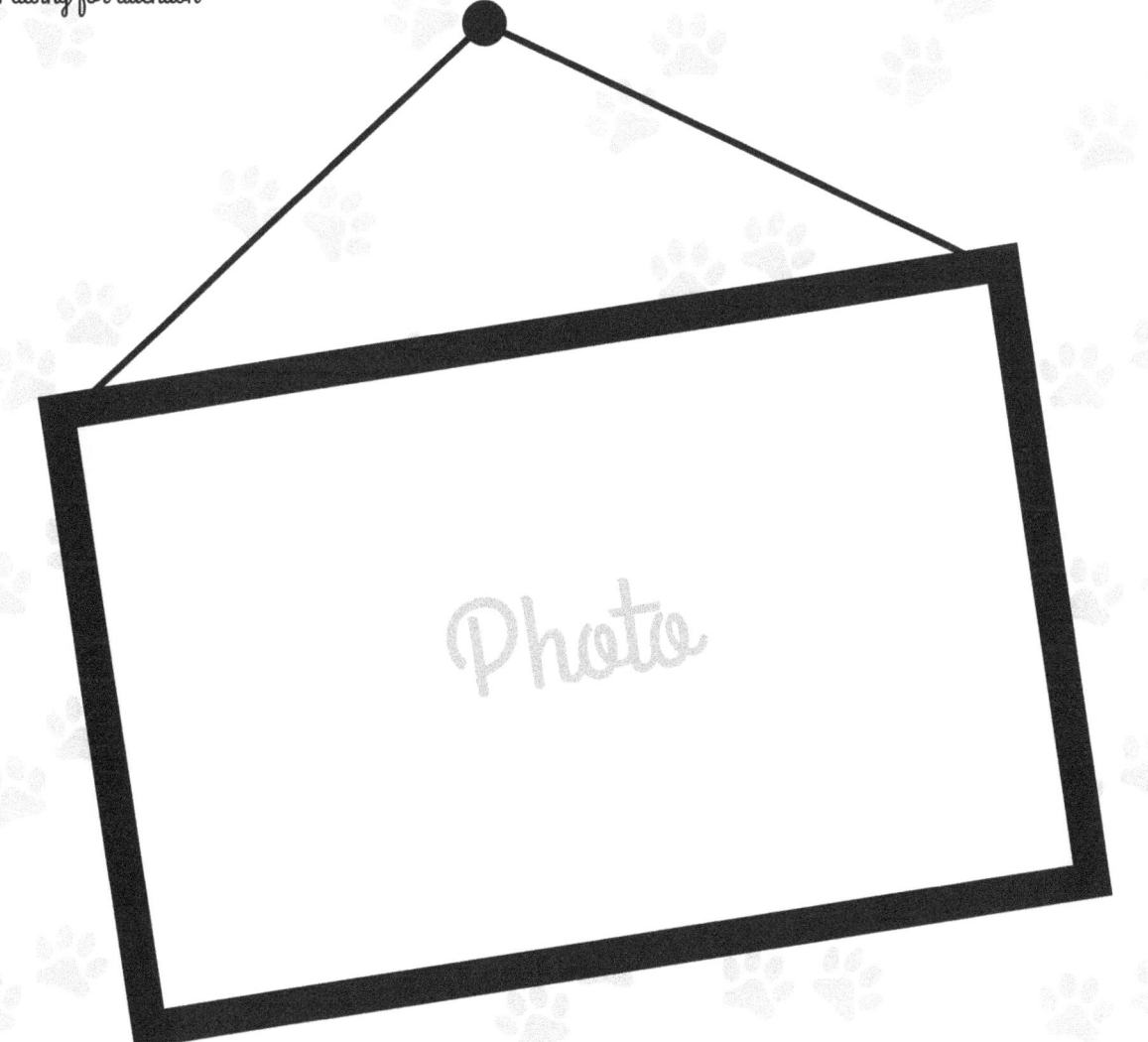

Letters to my dog in heaven

Dear Co-Woofer, thanks for being my supportive four-legged "co-worker" and I wanted to tell you that I love…

You were my favorite co-woofer, right now I'd like to tell you…

Today you make me happy by remembering your favorite…

Today, you make me happy by…

Your favorite dog park was… | Favorite place to get your dog bath was… | Your rating in the Snuggles department was… ☆☆☆☆☆

Your favorite toy was… | The times you made me laughed so hard were…

I found it funny when you… | I loved it when you… | When you rolled over, you…

On our "break time" from work, you loved to…

At the dog parked, you hate…

At the dog parked, you like..

Some lessons I learned from knowing you are…

Your favorite place to be scratched was…. | Favorite place to poop was…. | Your favorite place to nap was…

Favorite TV show was… | My "support system" includes… | You loved to torture the…

Things I loved

- [ ] Squeaky toys
- [ ] Bath time
- [ ] The vet
- [ ] Being a good boy
- [ ] Playtime at the dog park
- [ ] Chewy toys
- [ ] Dog bones
- [ ] Treats for being cute
- [ ] Rubbing tail in owner's face
- [ ] Pawing for attention
- [ ] Sitting on the keyboard
- [ ] Kissing my owner's neck
- [ ] "Meetings" with my new manager at home
- [ ] Holding my owner's paws
- [ ] Receiving the max amount of petting i can get
- [ ] Personal lap warmer
- [ ] Gossiping with my co-woofer
- [ ] Trying to drink my owner's coffee while sitting on the laptop
- [ ] Accidentally adding bookmarks to my owner's computer because i want attention

Letters to my dog in heaven

Dear Co-Woofer, thanks for being my supportive four-legged "co-worker" and I wanted to tell you that I love...

You were my favorite co-woofer, right now I'd like to tell you...

Today you make me happy by remembering your favorite...

Today, you make me happy by...

Your favorite dog park was...

Favorite place to get your dog bath was...

Your rating in the Snuggles department was..
☆ ☆ ☆ ☆ ☆

Your favorite toy was...

The times you made me laughed so hard were...

I found it funny when you...

I loved it when you...

When you rolled over, you...

On our "break time" from work, you loved to...

At the dog parked, you hate...

At the dog parked, you like..

Some lessons I learned from knowing you are...

Your favorite place to be scratched was....

Favorite place to poop was....

Your favorite place to nap was...

Favorite TV show was...

My "support system" includes...

You loved to torture the...

Things I loved

- [ ] Squeaky toys
- [ ] Bath time
- [ ] The vet
- [ ] Being a good boy
- [ ] Playtime at the dog park
- [ ] Chewy toys
- [ ] Dog bones
- [ ] Treats for being cute
- [ ] Rubbing tail in owner's face
- [ ] Pawing for attention
- [ ] Sitting on the keyboard
- [ ] Kissing my owner's neck
- [ ] "Meetings" with my new manager at home
- [ ] Holding my owner's paws
- [ ] Receiving the max amount of petting i can get
- [ ] Personal lap warmer
- [ ] Gossiping with my co-woofer
- [ ] Trying to drink my owner's coffee while sitting on the laptop
- [ ] Accidentally adding bookmarks to my owner's computer because i want attention

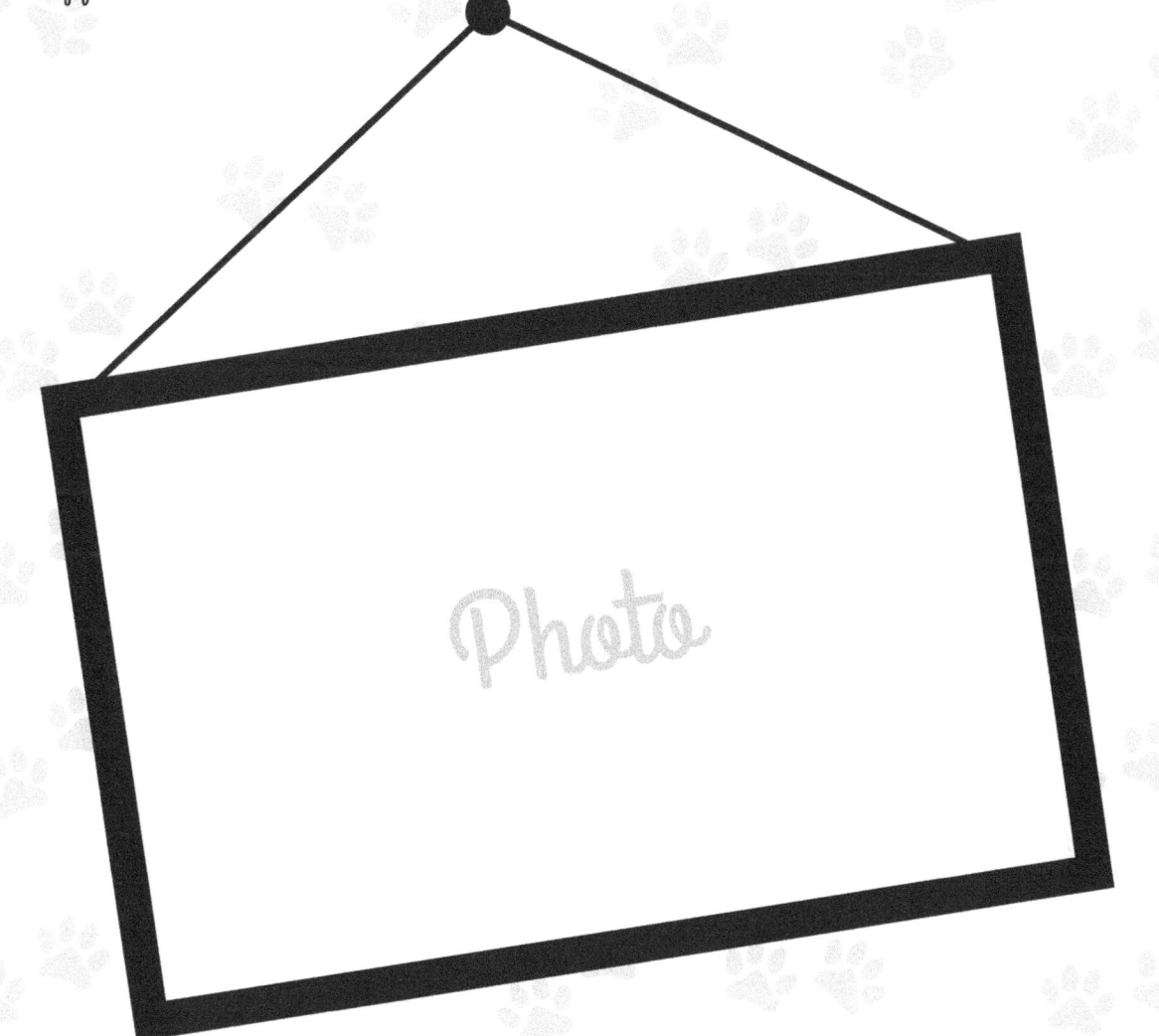

Letters to my dog in heaven

Dear Co-Woofer, thanks for being my supportive four-legged "co-worker" and I wanted to tell you that I love...

You were my favorite co-woofer, right now I'd like to tell you...

Today you make me happy by remembering your favorite...

Today, you make me happy by...

Your favorite dog park was...

Favorite place to get your dog bath was...

Your rating in the Snuggles department was...

☆☆☆☆☆

Your favorite toy was...

The times you made me laughed so hard were...

I found it funny when you...

I loved it when you...

When you rolled over, you...

On our "break time" from work, you loved to...

At the dog parked, you hate...

At the dog parked, you like..

Some lessons I learned from knowing you are...

Your favorite place to be scratched was....

Favorite place to poop was....

Your favorite place to nap was...

Favorite TV show was...

My "support system" includes...

You loved to torture the...

Things I loved

- ☐ Squeaky toys
- ☐ Bath time
- ☐ The vet
- ☐ Being a good boy
- ☐ Playtime at the dog park
- ☐ Chewy toys
- ☐ Dog bones
- ☐ Treats for being cute
- ☐ Rubbing tail in owner's face
- ☐ Pawing for attention
- ☐ Sitting on the keyboard
- ☐ Kissing my owner's neck
- ☐ "Meetings" with my new manager at home
- ☐ Holding my owner's paws
- ☐ Receiving the max amount of petting i can get
- ☐ Personal lap warmer
- ☐ Gossiping with my co-woofer
- ☐ Trying to drink my owner's coffee while sitting on the laptop
- ☐ Accidentally adding bookmarks to my owner's computer because i want attention

Letters to my dog in heaven

Dear Co-Woofer, thanks for being my supportive four-legged "co-worker" and I wanted to tell you that I love...

You were my favorite co-woofer, right now I'd like to tell you...

Today you make me happy by remembering your favorite...

Today, you make me happy by...

Your favorite dog park was...

Favorite place to get your dog bath was...

Your rating in the Snuggles department was...
☆ ☆ ☆ ☆ ☆

Your favorite toy was...

The times you made me laughed so hard were...

I found it funny when you...

I loved it when you...

When you rolled over, you...

On our "break time" from work, you loved to...

At the dog parked, you hate...

At the dog parked, you like..

Some lessons I learned from knowing you are...

Your favorite place to be scratched was....

Favorite place to poop was....

Your favorite place to nap was...

Favorite TV show was...

My "support system" includes...

You loved to torture the...

Things I loved

- [ ] Squeaky toys
- [ ] Bath time
- [ ] The vet
- [ ] Being a good boy
- [ ] Playtime at the dog park
- [ ] Chewy toys
- [ ] Dog bones
- [ ] Treats for being cute
- [ ] Rubbing tail in owner's face
- [ ] Pawing for attention
- [ ] Sitting on the keyboard
- [ ] Kissing my owner's neck
- [ ] "Meetings" with my new manager at home
- [ ] Holding my owner's paws
- [ ] Receiving the max amount of petting i can get
- [ ] Personal lap warmer
- [ ] Gossiping with my co-woofer
- [ ] Trying to drink my owner's coffee while sitting on the laptop
- [ ] Accidentally adding bookmarks to my owner's computer because i want attention

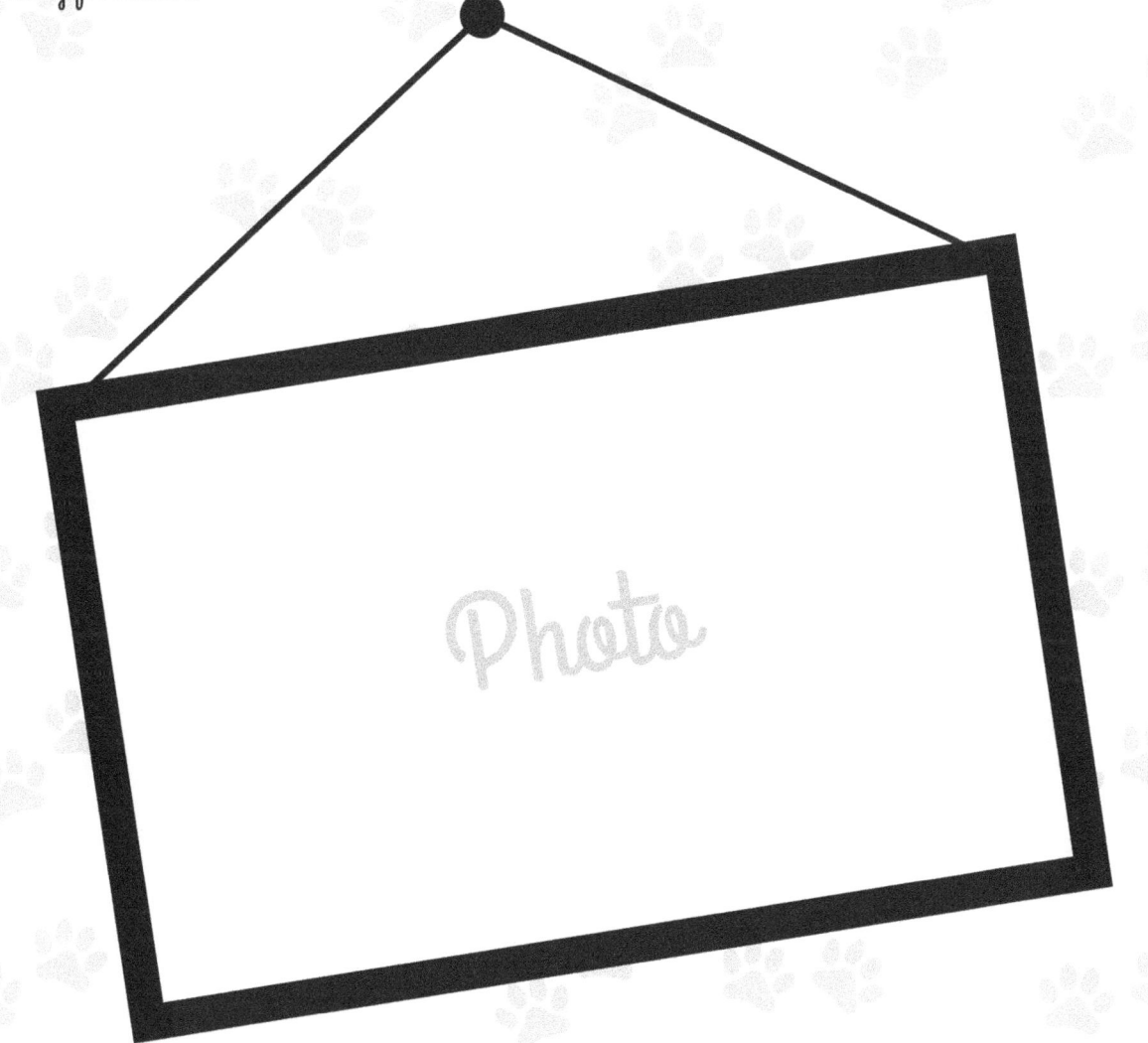

Letters to my dog in heaven

Dear Co-Woofer, thanks for being my supportive four-legged "co-worker" and I wanted to tell you that I love…

You were my favorite co-woofer, right now I'd like to tell you…

Today you make me happy by remembering your favorite…

Today, you make me happy by…

Your favorite dog park was…   Favorite place to get your dog bath was…   Your rating in the Snuggles department was…
☆ ☆ ☆ ☆ ☆

Your favorite toy was…   The times you made me laughed so hard were…

I found it funny when you…   I loved it when you…   When you rolled over, you…

On our "break time" from work, you loved to…

At the dog parked, you hate…

At the dog parked, you like..

Some lessons I learned from knowing you are…

Your favorite place to be scratched was….   Favorite place to poop was….   Your favorite place to nap was…

Favorite TV show was…   My "support system" includes…   You loved to torture the…

Things I loved

- [ ] Squeaky toys
- [ ] Bath time
- [ ] The vet
- [ ] Being a good boy
- [ ] Playtime at the dog park
- [ ] Chewy toys
- [ ] Dog bones
- [ ] Treats for being cute
- [ ] Rubbing tail in owner's face
- [ ] Pawing for attention
- [ ] Sitting on the keyboard
- [ ] Kissing my owner's neck
- [ ] "Meetings" with my new manager at home
- [ ] Holding my owner's paws
- [ ] Receiving the max amount of petting i can get
- [ ] Personal lap warmer
- [ ] Gossiping with my co-woofer
- [ ] Trying to drink my owner's coffee while sitting on the laptop
- [ ] Accidentally adding bookmarks to my owner's computer because i want attention

Letters to my dog in heaven

Dear Co-Woofer, thanks for being my supportive four-legged "co-worker" and I wanted to tell you that I love...

You were my favorite co-woofer, right now I'd like to tell you...

Today you make me happy by remembering your favorite...

Today, you make me happy by...

Your favorite dog park was...

Favorite place to get your dog bath was...

Your rating in the Snuggles department was ☆ ☆ ☆ ☆ ☆

Your favorite toy was...

The times you made me laughed so hard were...

I found it funny when you...

I loved it when you...

When you rolled over, you...

On our "break time" from work, you loved to...

At the dog parked, you hate...

At the dog parked, you like..

Some lessons I learned from knowing you are...

Your favorite place to be scratched was....

Favorite place to poop was....

Your favorite place to nap was...

Favorite TV show was...

My "support system" includes...

You loved to torture the...

Things I loved

- [ ] Squeaky toys
- [ ] Bath time
- [ ] The vet
- [ ] Being a good boy
- [ ] Playtime at the dog park
- [ ] Chewy toys
- [ ] Dog bones
- [ ] Treats for being cute
- [ ] Rubbing tail in owner's face
- [ ] Pawing for attention
- [ ] Sitting on the keyboard
- [ ] Kissing my owner's neck
- [ ] "Meetings" with my new manager at home
- [ ] Holding my owner's paws
- [ ] Receiving the max amount of petting i can get
- [ ] Personal lap warmer
- [ ] Gossiping with my co-woofer
- [ ] Trying to drink my owner's coffee while sitting on the laptop
- [ ] Accidentally adding bookmarks to my owner's computer because i want attention

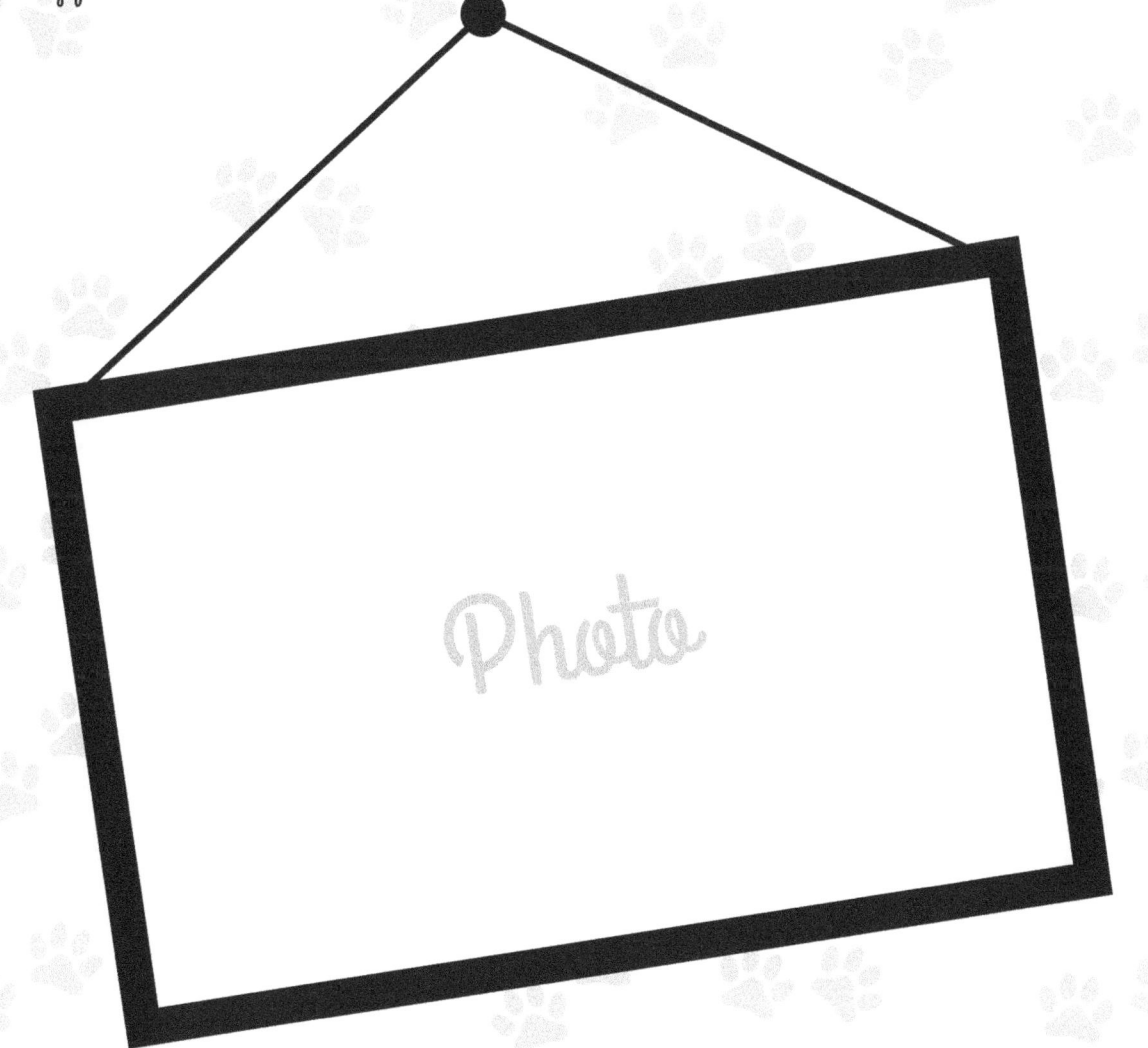

Lightning Source UK Ltd.
Milton Keynes UK
UKHW051611170720
366640UK00018B/1030